50
SIMPLE
THINGS
YOUR
BUSINESS
CAN DO TO
SAVE THE
EARTH

The EarthWorks Group

EarthWorks Press, Inc.
Berkeley, California

To Jesse. It's all his business.

THIS BOOK IS PRINTED ON RECYCLED PAPER.

Created and Packaged by Javnarama
Designed by Javnarama

ISBN 1-879682-02-8
First Edition 10 9 8 7 6 5 4 3 2 1

We've provided a great deal of information about
practices and products in our book. In most cases,
we've relied on advice, recommendations, and research
by others whose judgments we consider accurate and
free from bias. However, we can't and don't guarantee
the results. This book offers you a start.
The responsibility for using it
ultimately rests with you.

Quantity discounts and special editions are available.
For information, please contact:
Earthworks Press
1400 Shattuck Avenue, Box 25
Berkeley, CA 94709

Distributed to the book trade by Publisher's Group West

ACKNOWLEDGMENTS

The EarthWorks Group would like to thank everyone who worked with us to make this book possible, including:

- Joel Makower
- John Javna
- Fritz Springmeyer
- Nancy Tienvieri
- Carol Dana
- Kerry Hannon
- Laura Clark
- Francine Joselowsky
- Carla Garrison
- Dale Kondik
- Elizabeth Pollock
- Gail Mayville, Ben & Jerry's
- Miriam Kniaz, Business Ethics
- Matthew Costello, Corporation Conservation
- A.J. Grant, Environmental Communications Associates
- Rick Heede, Michael Shepard, Rocky Mountain Institute
- Patti Glikbarg
- Wayne Berman, U.S. Department of Transportation
- John Banta, Safe Environments
- Michael Silverstein
- Randy J. Rosenberg
- Kalman Stein
- Linda Ladas, Solar Energy Industries Association
- Cameron D. Beers, The Gillette Company
- Sally Randal
- Suzanne Gripman, Corporate Recycling Inc.
- Robin Kipke Alkire
- Melanie Foster
- Lenna Lebovich
- Catherine Dee
- John Dollison
- Lyn Speakman
- Nancy Evans
- Julie Bennett
- Reddy Kilowatt

CONTENTS

INTRODUCTION

I t has been a year since *50 Simple Things You Can Do to Save the Earth* sold its millionth copy. At the time, we were surprised to see that a substantial number of the books had been purchased by businesses. Then we realized things had changed. Businesses and environmentalists were no longer on opposite sides; we were all looking for ways to help keep our planet alive.

So now we've created an environmental book that specifically addresses the concerns of businesses.

We recognize that everyone in business—regardless of the position you hold in your company—has considerable influence over what happens to the environment. Each of you has a say in decisions that directly affect the state of the Earth...and the way people feel about taking care of it.

If, for example, you're responsible for purchasing supplies or products, you influence your vendors. Should they provide products that are better for the planet? You can help them decide by using your economic clout.

If you have a hand in building your company's image, you influence the way management—and the rest of the company—feels about the environment. Do people really care? Are they really getting the message? You can use your communications skills to spread the word.

If you manage production, you may be able to choose between toxic and nontoxic materials, and to influence methods of disposal.

If you work in an office, a workshop, a factory, you are the backbone of your company. You and co-workers can use your collective influence to mold policy decisions.

Of course, each of you have decisions to make each day. Should you throw out that piece of paper...or recycle it? Is it too much trouble to wash out a mug so you don't have to use a disposable cup? Should you leave a light or a copier running...or turn it off?

But in the end, it comes down to something quite simple: Business success is directly linked to the health of the Earth and its resources, including human resources. By taking some of the positive steps we've outlined in this book, you'll be making an investment . in the future.

The payoff on these investment isn't necessarily longterm. As you'll see, many of the ideas we've described in this book can yield dividends in this fiscal year—in cost savings, lower taxes, improved company image, and in increased employee satisfaction and productivity. This is a textbook case of "doing well by doing good."

Not all of these "simple things" will be right for your company. Big companies' needs are different from small companies'; businesses which own their own facilities have different needs from those that lease them; and industrial companies have different needs from retail and service businesses.

And you probably won't be able to implement more than a few of these things at once. In fact, if you take on too many "simple things" right away, you may lack the resources and support to make them work. So take it slowly, one idea at a time. As you build experience and confidence, other steps will follow naturally and easily.

We recognize the realities of business. We know it's not possible to turn well-honed products and processes topsy-turvy to protect the environment and still function as a business. But we have no doubt that being an environmentally responsible corporate citizen will give you a competitive advantage in the marketplace for years to come. And we know you want to save the Earth.

The EarthWorks Group,
March 17, 1991

SIMPLE

THINGS

1. MUG SHOT

Americans toss out enough paper and plastic cups, stirrers, spoons and forks every year to circle the equator 300 times.

Y ou take one last sip of coffee and make a hook shot into the trash can. Now it's time to get down to work. Sound familiar? It probably does—the average American office worker goes through around 500 disposable cups every year.

THE DISPOSABLE BLUES

• All those empty cups don't just disappear. Most plastic coffee cups are made of polystyrene foam—which never decomposes, no matter where you dump it.

• Paper cups don't break down easily, either. In fact, in a landfill— where most disposables end up—almost nothing breaks down. It just sits there.

• Both types of disposables use resources and create pollution. For example: Styrofoam is made from a carcinogenic oil byproduct called benzene. And paper cups are bleached, a process which puts toxic dioxins into our waterways.

• Styrofoam cups are touted by the plastics industry as "recyclable." Technically, that's true. But practically speaking, that's stretching it. There are few recycling facilities; and cups don't get recycled into more cups—so recycling doesn't reduce pollution or resource consumption.

SIMPLE THINGS TO DO

• Consider issuing each employee a ceramic mug, perhaps with your company logo or an environmental message printed on the side.

• Or keep sturdy mugs, not plastic cups, near the office coffee pot or eating area.

• Don't buy plastic stirrers—just keep some spoons on hand.

• If there's space to wash dishes, consider making durable plastic dishes available for employee use.

• Arrange for your cafeteria or coffee shop to give a discount to em-

Several magazines have a program called "Green Pages": They pledge to

ployees who bring their own mug when buying a cup of coffee.

• Arrange with owners of nearby carry-outs to give discounts to employees who bring their own mugs. If they have a salad bar, see if they'll let employees bring their own dishes or plastic containers instead of using the restaurant's disposable dishes.

SUCCESS STORY

• In 1990, Schnuck Markets in St. Louis stopped handing out free styrofoam cups. All 500 employees received a white ceramic coffee mug with the company's logo printed on the side. Now employees who want plastic must pay for it. Of course not everyone uses a mug; but according to food service manager Barb Vogel, the company still cuts out 2,000 plastic cups a month.

THE BOTTOM LINE

For Your Company

• Ceramic mugs cost about $2.50 each in bulk. Styrofoam cups cost about $3.35 per year per employee, assuming each person uses *only* one per day. But most employees use more than that. So mugs will pay for themselves in less than a year.

For The Earth

• If 10 million people used their own ceramic mugs in the office each day, we could eliminate as many as five billion cups.

• Lined up end to end, that's a savings of around 166 feet of landfill space per person per year—or a total of some 312,500 miles of trash a year.

RESOURCES

• **Greenpeace**, 1636 U St. NW, Washington, DC 20009. (202) 462-1177. *They sell mugs printed with environmental messages.*

• **ABCO Corporation**, 7401-V Fullerton Rd., Springfield, VA 22153. (703) 451-6700. *They sell mugs in bulk and take phone orders.*

• *Check in the Yellow Pages under "Restaurant Supply" for local sources of mugs.*

plant as many trees as they use to print their publications.

2. GREEN EGGS & HAM

*Nearly 44 million American workers purchase or
eat lunch out every weekday.*

I sn't it amazing how much junk is left after you eat a cafeteria lunch? There's a small mound of napkins, cups, utensils, plates, wrappers, coffee stirrers and so on. And that doesn't even include the leftover food.

But it doesn't take a lot of effort to trim your cafeteria's "wasteline." The results can be good for your company's bottom line, too.

OUT TO LUNCH
• Cafeterias and other food service institutions create about 8% of America's municipal waste—almost 13 million tons a year.

• According to a recent study, typical cafeteria waste consists of: paper (40%), food (23%), plastic (13%), polystyrene foam (10%), tin (8%), glass (5%) and aluminum (1%).

• It's estimated that more than 1/3 of this waste is recyclable.

• That includes the food. Some companies are beginning to compost their leftovers, which keeps them out of landfills.

SIMPLE THINGS TO DO
In the Company Cafeteria
• **Reduce packaging.** Check with vendors to see if your cafeteria's purchases can be delivered in fewer, larger cartons.

• **Buy recycled and unbleached paper products**—towels, napkins, coffee filters, etc. Bleaching can produce dioxins, which pollute water and may leave traces in the paper.

• **Whenever possible, use reusable plates, cups and silverware.** Disposables are a last resort, but if you buy them, check to see what can be recycled locally.

• **Use soft drink, milk, cream and condiment dispensers** instead of individual cans, cartons and packets.

• **Donate excess food** to a local shelter for the homeless or needy.

According to *The Green Consumer Letter*, U.S. companies introduced

- **Post your "lunchroom environmental policy"** where everyone can see it.
- **Encourage recycling.** Keep bins handy so employees can easily recycle after eating. And let them bring recyclables from home; it can help your recycling center break even...or even make a profit.

Work With Local Restaurants

- Ask local restaurant owners to give your employees a discount if they bring their own coffee mugs.
- When you have food delivered to meetings, ask restaurants to "hold the disposables." Use your own utensils, etc.

SUCCESS STORY

- The Levi Strauss cafeteria in San Francisco buys recycled paper trays and dishes. Diners are also asked to sort paper and aluminum for recycling. Some steps—like the use of recycled paper—actually cost the company more. "But we're doing it because we believe it needs to be done," says communications manager Dave Samson. "And the cafeteria is a place where we can make an immediate difference." Employee morale also gets a boost, he adds.

THE BOTTOM LINE

For Your Company

- You probably won't save any money here. The biggest benefit from creating a "green" lunchroom is what it does for your company's image ... and employees' self-image. Of course, there's a possibility that costs may be offset through reduced trash hauling costs and cafeteria recycling programs. But there's no guarantee.

For the Earth

- Reusing and recycling saves resources. If half of all company cafeterias reduced their trash by just 10%, we could eliminate 650,000 tons of trash a year.

RESOURCES

- **National Restaurant Association,** 1200 17th St. NW, Washington, DC 20036. (202) 331-5900.
- **Society for Food Service Management,** 304 W. Liberty St., Louisville, KY 40202. (502) 583-3783.

more than 2,700 "green" products in 1990.

3. COPY RIGHT

*Americans make nearly 400 billion photocopies a year—
about 750,000 copies every minute of every day.*

No doubt about it—Americans are "copy-holics." Our fingers itch at the thought of running off copies of everything from newspaper articles to inter-office memos. Sure, we've all seen the trash cans overflowing with unwanted copies.... But we just can't control ourselves.... We've *got* to make *just one more copy.*
Well, don't panic. There's help for our habit.

COPY MANIA
• There are more than 7 million copiers in operation in the United States, up from 4 million in 1987. By 1994, there will be an estimated 9 million machines.

• According to one expert, the average 100-person company uses about 378,000 sheets of copier paper a year. That's a stack of paper stretching nearly seven stories high.

SIMPLE THINGS TO DO
Save Paper
• Try copying on both sides of the paper. It could cut your paper use in half.

• Keep a collection box next to the copier for discarding bad copies. Put a sign near the copier asking employees to use the box. Use the discards as scrap or send it to your recycling center.

• Use recycled copying paper. A growing number of office supply stores stock it.

Save Energy
• If the machine is used infrequently, turn it off when it's not in use. Even an idle copier uses a surprising amount of electricity.

• If your copier is often left on all night, consider getting a timer that will shut the machine off between, say, 8 p.m. and 8 a.m.

If You're Buying a Copier
• Check out a duplex machine (which does two-sided copying).

Herman Miller burns its wood waste to generate steam and electricity to

• Select a copier with a power-saver feature. It can cut energy use more than elevenfold—from 7,600 watts to only 675 watts. If the copier is only used during 20% of the day, you could save over $900 a year in electricity costs.

SUCCESS STORY

• In 1987, Gail Mayville, environmental program development manager at Ben & Jerry's Homemade, got management to buy high-speed duplex (2-sided) copiers. Signs posted at the copy machines urge workers to reduce paper usage. According to Mayville, the company has saved thousands of reams of paper and has more than justified the purchase price. "No doubt about it, it works," says Mayville.

THE BOTTOM LINE
For Your Company

• You can cut copier paper usage by as much as 50%. If your company makes 5,000 copies a month, cutting paper use in half would save 30,000 sheets a year, or about $300 worth of paper.

• Energy-efficiency measures can save even more money. (See Turn It Off, page 46).

For the Earth

• If each copier in the U.S. used five fewer copies every business day, we could save up to 17.5 million reams of paper. That would save the equivalent of 1.4 million trees and keep more than 26 million cubic feet of paper out of landfills.

• If just 10% of our office copiers had power-saving features—or were simply turned off when not in use—we could save an estimated 7 billion kilowatt hours of electricity, the energy equivalent of 4 million barrels of oil a year.

RESOURCES

Try a local paper distributor. If they don't have it, contact:

• **Conservatree,** 10 Lombard Street, San Francisco, CA 94111. (415) 433-1000.

• **Quill Corp.,** (708) 634-4800 (East of the Rocky Mountains), (714) 988-3200 (West of the Rockies).

heat and cool its plant, saving $500,000 a year in fuel costs.

4. JUST THE FAX

*According to MCI, U.S. fax machines sent
30 billion faxes in 1990.*

"I'll fax it to you" has become as much a part of American business as "Your check is in the mail." It seems that just about everyone has access to a facsimile machine these days … so everyone has to cope with those curled-up pieces of shiny paper coming in at all hours of the day and night.

Faxing itself isn't bad. It uses less energy than other methods of sending documents and eliminates the need for envelopes, labels, and stamps.

But it's how you fax that makes a difference.

FAX FACTS

• Americans go through an estimated 300 million rolls of fax paper every year— enough to stretch from the earth to the moon 26 times.

• Unfortunately, standard fax paper isn't generally recyclable. It's coated with chemicals that are heated to create the printed images on a fax. These chemicals contaminate the recycling process.

• Because the chemicals deteriorate, faxes can fade after about six months. To save them, people often make photocopies—which wastes even more paper.

• Experts estimate that about one in four faxes gets photocopied.

SIMPLE THINGS TO DO

• **Buy a plain paper fax.** They work like photocopiers or laser printers; the faxes come out on plain paper and don't fade—which eliminates extra photocopying and enables you to recycle unneeded faxes. They aren't cheap—some sell for over $3,000—but prices are expected to drop to around $1,000 for the cheapest models.

• **Buy recycled thermal fax paper.** It sells for about $4.70 a roll.

Reducing the temperature of hot air blowing through heating ducts by

• **Use smaller cover sheets.** Instead of using a full page, use a half page. If you send five faxes a day, you'll save the equivalent of six rolls of paper in a year.

• **Or don't use a cover sheet at all.** You can buy Post-It fax-transmission stickers. Stick it on the first page before you send it.

THE BOTTOM LINE

For Your Company

• Plain paper fax machines are more expensive to buy, but less expensive to use. Faxes cost about three cents each, compared with about six cents for a thermal fax. But plain paper models also require toner and developer, which add to their operation cost. In the end, the cost of the two machines is pretty close—but the quality of the plain paper fax makes it a much better buy.

For the Earth

• If everyone who owns a fax machine switched from full-page to half-page cover sheets, we could save about 2   million miles worth of unrecyclable fax paper—without reducing the number of faxes.

• If one in 10 fax users switched to a plain paper fax, and those faxes were recycled, we could save an additional 500,000 miles of paper.

RESOURCES

Plain Paper Fax Machines

• **Canon Business Machines,** 3191 Red Hill Ave., Costa Mesa, CA 92626. (714) 556-4700.

• **Sharp Electronics Corp.,** Sharp Plaza, Mahwah, NJ 07495. (201) 529-8200.

• **Quill Corp.** (708) 634-4800 (East of the Rocky Mountains) or (714) 988-3200 (West of the Rockies). They plan to introduce a low-priced plain paper fax machine.

Recycled Fax Paper

• **Paper Systems Inc.,** 185 Pioneer Rd., Springboro, OH 45066. (800) 950-8590. They sell recycled fax paper.

• **Rite Made Paper,** 1501 W 29th St., Kansas City, MO 64108.

by five degrees can save $30,000 for a 100,000 square foot building.

5. CHECKS & BALANCES

American businesses charged over $60 billion to credit cards in 1990.

"**A**nd how will you be paying for that?"
Every time you charge something on a company credit card or write a company check, you could be using a little bit of your spending power to support environmental groups.

CHARGE IT

• Whenever you use your Visa or MasterCard, the retailer pays a small processing fee to the bank that issued the card.

• Visa and MasterCard have a service called "affinity cards," which makes it possible for environmental groups to get a portion of every processing fee.

• Once an environmental group signs up with the credit card company, a part of each "affinity card" purchase goes to that group. It may only be a few cents per charge, but it adds up.

• How much? In 1990, the Environmental Defense Fund's Nature Card earned the organization $125,000.

• There's a similar program for check writers. Every time you order a certain brand of checks, money is donated to a participating environmental group. The checks also have the organization's logo on them.

• You can use the checks no matter where you bank.

SIMPLE THINGS TO DO

• **Switch your company credit card to an "affinity card."** Contact Visa or MasterCard for a list of affinity programs that benefit environmental groups.

• **Check with environmental organizations you want to support.** See if they have an "affinity card" program. Many large groups (e.g., the Audubon Society, Sierra Club, etc.) do.

• **Don't stop with company accounts.** Tell employees about "affinity" services. They may want to switch, too.

At Coca Cola's Atlanta headquarters, employees can bring in

• **Have your company buy checks that support environmental organizations.** Note: These checks aren't available in formats suitable for larger businesses yet.

SUCCESS STORIES
• The Working Assets Visa Card, with about 100,000 cardholders, generated over $500,000 in donations in 1990. The money was divided among 12 different environmental groups, working on issues like hazardous waste, wildlife protection, nuclear safety, rain-forest preservation, transportation policy, energy conservation and protecting the environment in the Soviet Union.

THE BOTTOM LINE
For Your Company
• Switching to affinity credit cards and message checks won't cost your company much (if anything), but it can raise millions for groups working to save the Earth. Environmentally conscious employees will appreciate this show of concern; it can increase their motivation and commitment to your company.

For the Earth
• U.S. environmental groups received about $7.3 million in donations in 1990. If American businesses put just 3% of company charges on affinity credit cards, we could double that amount.

RESOURCES
• **Message! Check Corp.,** P.O. Box 3206, Seattle, WA 98114. (206) 324-7792.

• **Visa USA, Corporate Relations,** P.O. Box 8999, San Francisco, CA 94128. (415) 570-3814.

• **MasterCard International,** Attn: Stephen Drees, 888 Seventh Ave., New York, NY 10106. (212) 649-4600.

recyclables from home to deposit in the company's bins.

6. CUT PAPER

By the year 2000, U.S. businesses will be filing 120 billion sheets of new paper a year—enough to fill 5 million file cabinets.

Maybe you didn't need to send a copy of that last memo to everybody, but you wanted to make sure no one was left out.

And wouldn't you know it—the only paper handy when you had to jot down that phone number was a new piece of stationery.

We all use more paper than we need to. But there are plenty of ways to cut down.

DID YOU KNOW

• U.S. businesses now use about 21 million tons of paper every year. That's about 175 pounds for each American.

• According to one estimate, more than 350 million trees are cut down each year to make office paper.

• We throw away enough office paper every year to build a 12-foot high-wall from New York City to Los Angeles.

• Each ton of paper thrown away can cost about $100 to discard and uses three cubic feet of landfill space.

• According to the Conservatree Paper Company, about 70% of all office trash is wastepaper that could be recycled.

SIMPLE THINGS TO DO

• **Use both sides of the paper.** It's increasingly common for letters and reports to be written on both the front and back sides.

• **Cut down on memos.** Just post a few copies where people will see them—around the coffee room, bathrooms, elevators, etc.

• **Set up a bulletin board** on every floor or in each department for notices and memos.

• **Consider using electronic mail** for interoffice memos (if you have a networked computer system). Many systems can pay for themselves through reduced paper use.

According to the Rocky Mountain Institute, it takes the energy equivalent of about

• **Use scrap paper.** If you have outdated letterhead, reports, or other unneeded paper that's printed on one side, turn it into scratch paper. A local print shop can cut it to any size and glue it into scratch pads. Some companies will even print "From the Desk of..." before turning it into pads.

SUCCESS STORY
• The staff of *New Woman* magazine cut its paper use by recycling old paper for memos. "We've made our employees much more aware of the waste we generate," says Dirk Vonderlage, an editorial aide. "Until now, there's been an attitude that 'Only a brand new sheet of paper is worthy of writing my notes on,' rather than using a piece of scratch paper."

THE BOTTOM LINE
For Your Company
• Using less paper costs nothing, but it can save money and trash hauling fees. If employees in a typical 50 person office use both sides of the paper only 10% of the time, the company could save $750 a year just in reduced paper costs.

For the Earth
• If all employees reduced paper use by just 5%, we could save over a million tons of paper each year, enough to save about 17 million trees. It also reduces the air and water pollution generated by making new paper.

RESOURCE
• *The Greenpeace Guide to Paper*. Send $3 to Greenpeace Northwest, 4649 Sunnyside Ave. N, Seattle, WA 98103.

75,000 tons of coal a year just to power our nation's fax machines.

7. USE GREENER CLEANERS

According to the EPA, many of the 100 chemical pollutants found in sewage systems come from institutional cleaners.

When you clean at home, you know what products you're using because ... well ... *you're* using them. But at work, everything gets clean "magically." When you arrive there in the morning, the trash has been taken out, the bathrooms are spotless, the floor has been scrubbed.

What about the cleaning supplies it took to get the job done? They may be harmful to the environment and to you. It's worth having your company look into it.

DIRTY BUSINESS
• Many commercial cleaning products contain toxic, corrosive or flammable chemicals like perchloroethylene, napthalene, sodium hypochlorite, toluene and benzene.
• Many of these ingredients get washed down drains and into sewage systems. They're supposed to break down or be filtered out in wastewater treatment plants, but that doesn't always happen. The result: Toxins get into the water supply.
• Many cleaners use chlorine as a disinfectant. In waste water, chlorine can react with organic and other compounds to create toxins or carcinogens.
• That's not all. The fumes from these products also cause pollution indoors. Some irritate people's eyes, noses and lungs.

SUCCESS STORIES
• Sheraton Grande Hotel in LA switched to Con-Lei cleaner. It let them eliminate hazardous acid-based cleaners for their floors.
• The University of California, Davis, uses 1 oz. of Con-Lei per gallon of water to clean just about everything. According to the custodial manager, "Employee acceptance is high due to the cleaning abilities of the product, as well as the lack of strong odor or irritation to the skin."

To reduce smog, Los Angeles businesses with over 100 employees must offer

• Another product, Bioclean, a bulk concentrated institutional cleaner, is used at Big Chief Lodge in Indiana. "It works well on mildew, carpet stains, showers and tubs, and in the kitchen areas where odor is a problem," says general manager Robert L. Boyer.

SIMPLE THINGS TO DO
• Use cleaners that won't harm people or the environment. They aren't usually available from janitorial supply firms. You have to contact the manufacturers directly.

• Instead of buying one product to clean floors, another for glass, etc., look for all-purpose products. They let you buy bigger quantities of fewer products, saving money and reducing packaging.

• Look for concentrated cleaners. Concentrates give you more product for less packaging and use fewer resources being transported from factory to business. They usually cost less, too.

• Provide your maintenance staff with instructions on how to use greener cleaners. Many work differently than traditional products (e.g., some create fewer suds) and take a little getting used to. Ask the manufacturer for educational materials.

THE BOTTOM LINE
For Your Company
• Greener cleaners cost more to buy than other institutional cleaning products, but because they are usually concentrated, they can save money in the long run. Using Con-Lei allowed the Maricopa Medical Center to reduce manpower and cleaning supply costs. They cut their annual cleaning bill by almost 90%, from $4080 to only $480.

For the Earth
• Greener cleaners will cut the amount of harmful chemicals sent into the water supply.

RESOURCES
• **Chip Distribution Co.**, P.O. Box 704, Manhattan Beach, CA 90266. (213) 603-1114. *Makers of Con-Lei colloid cleaner*.
• **Natural Chemistry, Inc.**, 244 Elm St., New Canaan, CT 06840. (203) 966-8761. *They make Bioclean and other bulk concentrated institutional cleaners*.

employees $15 a month to take public transit instead of driving to work.

8. A PACKAGE DEAL

About a third of America's nonhazardous waste stream is packaging materials. That's enough to cover all of Philadelphia in a foot of paper.

I t's time to fill an order.

First, pull out a new corrugated box and secure the bottom with plastic packing tape. Now put the merchandise in a plastic bag and set it in the box; pour Styrofoam peanuts all around for protection. Finally, close the box and seal it with more tape. Don't forget to cover the address with extra tape ... just in case.

Congratulations.... You've just created an environmental nightmare. But don't feel boxed in; there are plenty of things you can do to clean up your packaging act.

PACK FACTS

• U.S. businesses use an estimated 5 billion cubic feet of Styrofoam "peanuts" a year—enough to fill the Empire State Building more than 135 times.

• Annually, we use the equivalent of 120 corrugated cardboard boxes for every person in America—enough to make a pile as big as a football field and as high as the World Trade Center.

• Every year, Americans send some 2 billion packages through the U.S. Postal Service, U.P.S. and Federal Express. That's eight for every man, woman and child in the country.

SIMPLE THINGS TO DO
When You Ship

• **Reuse items from old packages:** envelopes, boxes, Styrofoam "peanuts," etc. Devise a system for collecting the "peanuts" you receive; then send them to the shipping department for reuse. Some companies hang large trash bags in central locations.

• **Make your own packaging materials:** Run unrecyclable papers through a shredder. It works nicely to pack delicate objects.

• **Use real popcorn,** made with a hot-air popper. Some companies even buy bags of ready-made popcorn. Caution: Boxes packed with popcorn can attract pests. And even popcorn made with hot air contains oils, which can rub off onto packed goods.

RECYCLED & RECYCLABLE

- **Use paper packaging tape instead of plastic.** It makes boxes easier to recycle.
- **Buy roll ends** from local printers or newspapers for use as packing materials. Roll ends are the final few feet of a printer's roll of paper, which can't be used and are often thrown away.
- **Reuse manila envelopes.** Get a rubber stamp that says, "This envelope is being reused as part of our environmental commitment."
- **Check with local recyclers:** The adhesive on pressure-sensitive labels may make boxes and envelopes unrecyclable.
- **Use Jiffy Bags filled with recycled paper.** Shipping envelopes with bubble-pak inside are non-recyclable.
- **Enclose a note in your packages** asking recipients to reuse packing materials. Tilden Press in Washington, D.C. sends a note that says, "The packing material used in this shipment contains polystyrene we received in shipments sent to us by other companies. We are reusing it, and would appreciate your doing the same."
- **Ask suppliers** to use recycled and recyclable packing materials.

SUCCESS STORIES

- MacConnection, a New Hampshire mail order company, stocks a variety of box sizes so products fit tightly and need less packaging. It also switched from "peanuts" to newsprint, cutting trash by 75%.
- Backpacker's Pantry in California uses roll ends from a local newspaper. Seven rolls, which sell for $7, go as far as 1-1/2 bags of Styrofoam "peanuts," which cost $16.

RESOURCES

- **EcoPak Industries**, 7859 S 180th St., Kent, WA 98032. (206) 768-9600.
- **Bio-Pax**, 1265 Pine Hill Dr., Annapolis, MD 21401. (301) 974-4411. *Both of these companies make several types of recycled and recyclable packing materials. Write for their catalogs.*

saves over 6,000 pounds of chemicals a year from being discarded.

9. GO PUBLIC

*Sixty one million workers drive to work alone every day: That's
enough cars to form a convoy circling the globe seven times.*

Did you drive to work this morning?
How was it—was the road crowded? Were the parking
fees higher than your weekly paycheck? Did you have to
take out a second mortgage just to fill your gas tank?

Not everyone is lucky enough to have an alternative. But if you
live in an urban area, you probably do—you can take public transportation. It doesn't have all the conveniences of driving your
own car. But it doesn't have the headaches either. And the less
you drive, the better it is for the planet.

BREATHE EASIER

• Commuting by public transportation takes as little as one-
thirtieth the energy needed to commute by car.

• Each person who uses public transit instead of a private car
keeps an average of 9.1 pounds of smog-producing hydrocarbons,
62 pounds of carbon dioxide, and 5 pounds of nitrogen oxides
(which contribute to acid rain) out of the atmosphere every year.

SIMPLE THINGS TO DO

• **Offer bus and rail passes to employees at a discount.** (Some
transit systems sell companies passes at a discount, which can be
passed on to employees.) Better yet, give them away.

• **Provide a "transit allowance" to employees** who use public
transportation. It's a tax deduction for companies, and employees
can receive up to $15 a month in passes as a tax-free benefit.

• **Distribute copies of area public transit route maps** to employees. They're free from most transit agencies.

• **If your company isn't close to a public transit stop**, set up a
company shuttle bus (or van, or car) to take workers back and
forth. (See "Everybody Into the Pool.") Coordinate it with the ar-
rival of buses or trains to minimize waiting time.

IBM has had an environmental policy since 1971. Every product, process or

SUCCESS STORIES

- Geico, an insurance company in Bethesda, MD, buys reduced-price bus and rail passes for its employees, so they can take public transit for about half price. About 550 of the company's 2,500 employees participate. Another 450 receive $15 a month to take public transit one day a week, instead of driving.
- Atlantic Richfield offered employees $100 a month to take buses to work and was "overwhelmed" with the response.
- Under its "Our Clean Air" program, Total Petroleum Inc., a Denver oil company, offered customers free bus passes with a fill-... for use on high pollution days. Over 15,000 people got passes

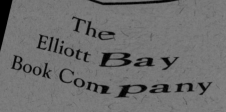

... n helps cut the cost of moving people

...ed to parking lots can be used more ...purposes.

...hat buy transit passes for employees re-

...ers left their cars at home one day a ...n gallons of gas a year and cut pollu-...ple: We'd keep 840 million pounds of

...n more than 100 employees operated a ...e 900,000 commuting cars off the ...number that commute into the Wash-...rea during rush hour.

...er Transportation, 808 17th St. NW, ...)6. (202) 659-0602. *Publishes a bi-*
...*ing for members.*

possible effects on the environment.

10. THE CARTRIDGE FAMILY

American businesses throw out 15 million plastic toner cartridges every year, enough to stretch from New York to Zurich.

You probably hate it when the "low toner" light on your copier comes on, or you get to the end of your typewriter ribbon. Not only do you get your hands dirty changing it, you have to throw away a big chunk of plastic. There ought to be something you can do with it: An art project? Pencil holder? Paperweight? Actually, there's a simple solution: Fill it up again.

TONING UP

• Many photocopiers and laser printers use plastic toner cartridges that must be replaced occasionally—at $100 or more apiece. The cartridges contain the black substance that prints on the page. The more you print, the faster you use it up.

• But the plastic container doesn't wear out. It can be reused many times. The same is true for typewriter and printer ribbons. The ribbons run out, but the plastic casings are reusable.

• Laser printer and copier cartridges weigh about five pounds each. That means about 40,000 tons of plastic cartridges end up in landfills each year, not including printer ribbon cartridges.

• A growing industry of cartridge recyclers (or "rechargers") has emerged to refill cartridges. In 1989, about 3,000 rechargers refilled 1.5 million cartridges.

• Rechargers disassemble the cartridge or ribbon casing, inspect it, replace worn or broken parts, and clean everything. Then the toner is refilled or the ribbon replaced.

• Other companies "remanufacture" or "reload" new ribbons in used ribbon casings.

SIMPLE THINGS TO DO

Find a Recharger

• Look for a recharger in your area. Check a local computer maga-

Polaroid figured out how to reuse 50 gallon drums up to seven times by

zine, or the Yellow Pages under "Computer Supplies."

• If you can't find a recharging service in your area, or want to check a company's reputation, contact the American Cartridge Recycling Association (ACRA). (See Below.)

Collect empty cartridges and ribbons

• Make sure there are enough extras around so you'll have some to use while others are being recharged.

• Even if you don't recharge, some rechargers will take your empty cartridges and donate money to environmental groups in exchange. Call ACRA for referrals.

THE BOTTOM LINE

For Your Company

• Refilling a toner cartridge costs about $50—about half the cost of a new one.

• Bonus: Many rechargers refill cartridges with more toner than you get in a new cartridge. Many rechargers also provide free pickup and delivery or shipping.

• Ribbons can generally be reloaded at about 40% the price of a new one. The savings are greatest for companies doing high-volume printing with minicomputer or mainframes. Changing a minicomputer ribbon once a week could save you $600 a year.

• Another bonus: Because most new cartridges and ribbons are made in Japan, and most rechargers are local, recycling keeps jobs and money in the U.S.

For the Earth

• Besides saving trash, recharging also saves oil. The plastic used in cartridges contains about a half quart of oil. Recycling could save a million gallons of oil a year.

RESOURCE

• **American Cartridge Recycling Association**, 1717 N Bayshore Dr., Ste. 2434, Miami, FL 33132. (305) 539-0701. *They establish standards for rechargers and can recommend a qualified one in your area. They'll also refer you to rechargers who donate money to environmental groups in exchange for empty cartridges.*

lining them with vinyl. Before that, they threw them away after just one use.

11. THE BEST-LAID PLANTS

A study by NASA found that plants can remove up to 87% of toxic indoor air within 24 hours.

It's estimated that nearly a third of all new office buildings have indoor air quality problems. Everything from the copier to the carpet can give off hazardous gases.

The result? As one expert puts it, "When that dirty air is trapped and recirculated inside tightly-sealed, climate-controlled buildings, it's like bathing in somebody's used bathwater."

One simple way you can improve the air quality in your office is to bring in some plants.

A GROWING CONCERN

• A four-year U.S. Army study found that workers in modern, energy-efficient buildings were 50% more likely to get colds and contract respiratory infections than people in older buildings.

• Common office pollutants include: formaldehyde (given off by particle board, wall paneling, plywood, furniture and carpeting); trichloroethylene (from some inks, paints and varnishes); and benzene (from tobacco smoke, gasoline fumes, and some plastics, inks and oils).

• The good news: Plants can absorb these pollutants through leaves, roots and accompanying microorganisms. Then they convert the pollutants into food—the same process that nature uses to clean air outside.

SIMPLE THINGS TO DO

• Put air-cleaning plants around your workplace—even on the factory floor. Recommended: At least one four- to five-foot plant per 100 square feet.

• Some of the most effective: philodendrons, golden pothos, English ivy, peace lily, and mother-in-law's tongue. These plants can grow under fluorescent lights, as well as in front of windows. If you have more light, spider plants and flowering plants like chrysanthemums and azaleas work.

SUCCESS STORIES

• Ecotech Auto Works, a McLean, VA, car repair shop, hangs spider plants in its work area to absorb the exhaust fumes. "They feel right, look good and customers react favorably" says the company president. "Plants solidify their impression that we're a different kind of shop."

• At Progressive Brokers Ltd., a New Zealand insurance company, employees started to get sick and customers complained of eye irritations after new partitions were installed. When nothing else worked, they tried plants. In four months, the company had clean air. "At last we don't have health problems with our staff," says the manager.

THE BOTTOM LINE

For Your Company

• Indoor air pollution can cost your company plenty. A study reported in the *American Journal of Medicine* estimated that 150 million work days are lost every year due to upper respiratory problems— adding $15 billion a year in health care costs.

• It costs about $75,000 to put 1,000 plants in a 100,000 square foot office building occupied by 660 workers. Maintenance could run about $20,000 a year. If absenteeism dropped by just 1%, a company could save $165,000 in increased productivity the first year.

• Besides cleaning air, plants help create a more pleasant environment. That can raise morale, commitment and productivity.

For the Earth

• When we rely on "natural" solutions to address pollution problems, "we don't deplete energy or other resources that would be needed for 'higher tech' approaches," says the Foliage for Clean Air Council.

RESOURCES

• **Foliage for Clean Air Council,** 405 N Washington St., Falls Church, VA 22046. (703) 241-4004. *A clearinghouse on the use of plants to improve indoor air. Write for a free information packet.*

• **National Aeronautics and Space Administration**, Bldg. 2423, Stennis Space Center, MS 39529. *Ask for its study, "Interior Landscape Plants for Indoor Air Pollution Abatement."*

12. SUPPLIES & DEMANDS

"Our supplier relationships afford us the opportunity to extend our social mission into the business we do with them."
—Ben & Jerry's Homemade

You're doing your part at work to try to protect the environment.... But your suppliers don't seem to care.

What can you do?

Maybe it's time to use some of your "customer clout" to encourage them to change their policies.

MONEY TALKS

• In 1991, Ace Hardware Corp.'s paint division notified suppliers that it would be conducting audits of all vendors. The statement reads: "We reserve the right to immediately cancel any business awarded to a vendor found to be in non-compliance with any applicable federal, state or local regulations, or who ... shows blatant disregard for the best interest of our environment...." According to Tom Daley, head of Ace's paint division, "As we gain information from audits, it can be beneficial and even save us money."

SIMPLE THINGS TO DO

• Set up criteria for your vendors. But don't ask them to do anything that your company isn't already doing. For example, you might decide you won't accept packages containing styrofoam peanuts.

• Put your policy in writing and send it to the head of each company who would be affected by the policy.

• Be sure to apply rules uniformly. If you demand something of one company, you should demand the same thing of everyone else.

THE BOTTOM LINE

• Making demands of suppliers and vendors probably won't cost anything, but it sends a message that you're committed to changing the way American companies do business ... and to using your influence to protect the Earth.

About 15% of all pencils are made from wood harvested in endangered rainforests.

13. A GREEN CATALOG

Experts estimate that less than 3% of the office supplies Americans purchase annually are recycled ... or recyclable.

Here's an easy way to encourage people in your company to buy environmentally sound supplies: Put together your own catalog.

SIMPLE THINGS TO DO

• **Put together a "catalog" of eco-products** your company can use. It doesn't have to be fancy; just type it onto a few pieces of paper (both sides, of course).

• **Items to include:** recycled paper goods; office supplies made of recycled materials; durable products; "green" cleaners; recycling bins. If it fits your company's needs, include energy-efficient lighting, recycled motor oil, packing materials, and pallets.

• **List items by category.** Include product number, distributor's name, address, phone number and additional ordering info.

• **If possible, include a letter** from a company VIP requesting that buyers make an effort to purchase these products.

• **Your company's buying power** can help make environmentally sound products affordable—and encourage manufacturers to make a wider variety of them.

SUCCESS STORY

• In 1990, the management of Pacific Gas & Electric mandated a pro-environment buying policy for all its offices. To make compliance easier, the company put together a 12-page "Green Catalog" featuring paper products, cleaners, aerosol alternatives and printer and copier supplies. "Within the first few months, we had a five-fold increase in recycled or environmentally preferred materials," says Claude Poncelet, who heads the company's Corporate Environmental Initiative. "People are very enthusiastic about that. They appreciate having the information."

Spartan Stores uses a computer to plot delivery routes in order to save fuel.

14. INVEST IN THE EARTH

*In 1990, employee pension funds controlled around
18% of all the corporate stock in the U.S.*

Investment portfolios—including employee pension funds, the
extra capital your company may keep in reserve, and your own
personal investments—have tremendous power to help the
earth. How? By supporting companies with good environmental
records.

MONEY TALKS

• The total value of outstanding stock in U.S. corporations is
around $6.5 trillion. Pension funds hold around $1.3 trillion of
that—including more than 50% of the outstanding stocks in
America's largest corporations.

• Pension funds also own about 27% of all corporate bonds.

• Since 1984, Americans have invested more than $450 billion in
environmentally oriented and socially responsible corporations.

• These white knights include Yellow Freight System of Delaware,
Pitney Bowes, Quaker Oats, Rubbermaid and Snap-On Tools.

SIMPLE THINGS TO DO

Add the environment to your pension portfolio

• It's simple to add "green" investments, provided there's sufficient
interest among employees.

• The pension administrator will need a prospectus and annual report to determine any investment's potential.

Ask your employer to consider eco-investing

• Does your company invest its nonworking capital into a money
market or mutual fund that helps the environment? Read the company's annual report for information. This is usually listed on the
balance sheet as "Other investments" or "Securities." If you
work for a publicly traded company, the information should be
readily available. If you have problems, check with the firm's chief

Kellogg Co. encourages electronic mail, bulletin boards and

financial officer or the investor relations office.

• Be determined, but tactful. Most companies don't like giving out this kind of financial information, especially to employees.

THE BOTTOM LINE

For Your Company

• All financial investments have a risk factor. There is no hard evidence to suggest that these environmental funds are any more successful than any other well-managed ones. On the other hand, environmental regulations are getting more stringent all the time. Companies that prevent pollution will, over the long term, be better investments than companies that wait until costly cleanups are required.

For the Earth

• As a stockholder, you have a voice in setting company policy. By investing in environmentally responsible companies, you're using your voice—along with millions of other employees—to support companies that are helping the Earth.

RESOURCES

• **Calvert Social Investment Fund,** 4550 Montgomery Ave., Bethesda, MD 20814. (800) 368-2750.

• **Council on Economic Priorities,** 30 Irving Pl., New York, NY 10003. (212) 420-1133.

• **Directory of Environmental Investing,** Environmental Economics, 1026 Irving St., Phila., PA 19017. (215) 925-7168.

• **Directory of Socially Responsible Investments,** Funding Exchange, 666 Broadway, 5th Fl., N.Y., NY 10012. (212) 529-5300.

• **Investor Responsibility Research Center,** 1755 Massachusetts Ave. NW, Washington DC 20036. (202) 939-6500.

• **New Alternatives Fund,** 295 Northern Blvd., Great Neck, NY 11021. (516) 466-0808.

• **Social Investment Forum,** 430 First Ave. N, Ste. 290, Minneapolis, MN 55401. (612) 333-8338.

• **Working Assets,** 230 California St., San Francisco, CA 94111. (800) 533-3863.

single-spacing reports to reduce paper use.

15. REFLECT ON IT

The typical company has more fluorescent lights than employees.

A re you trying to conserve energy at work? Here's a simple way to save on lighting costs.

REFLECTIONS

• About half the light from a fluorescent tube is absorbed by the inside of the fixture.

• Reflectors redirect that "lost" light. The result: You can remove half the bulbs and ballasts and still get the same amount of light.

SIMPLE THINGS TO DO

• Install reflectors in overhead fluorescent fixtures. Many are simple to install. You only need to remove a couple of tubes and screw in the reflector.

• Experts suggest that you install electronic ballasts and new bulbs at the same time you put in reflectors. That provides maximum savings and allows you to do everything in one operation.

THE BOTTOM LINE

For Your Company

• Installing two reflectors, changing ballasts, and replacing bulbs costs about $75 per fixture—including labor. Each saves about $23 a year in reduced energy costs and lower maintenance. So the investment could pay for itself in about three years. Many utilities will pay rebates of 50% or more, cutting the payback time.

For the Earth

• If all fluorescent lighting fixtures used reflectors, we could save up to 356 billion kilowatt hours of electricity.

RESOURCE

• **Brauer Engineering,** 388 N Fratney St., Milwaukee, WI 53212. (414) 963-3030. *They make the WATT SAVR reflector.*

The staff at the Penta Hotel in NY has an unwritten rule to reduce paper use: No memos.

16. ON THE ROAD

*A single company car driven 1,000 miles a month can pump
6 tons of carbon dioxide into the atmosphere every year.*

"I t's not my car. Why should I worry about fuel efficiency?"
That's the attitude many of us have when we're behind the
wheel of a company car or one leased for a business trip.
But no matter who owns the car, the impact on the earth is the
same. So it's worth following a few basic guidelines. You'll cut
down on pollution ... and save money for your company, which
can translate into higher profits, bigger raises and happier bosses.

Maybe you'll even pick up a few tips to use on your own car.

YOU AUTO KNOW
• A car gets as much as 20% better gas mileage at 55 miles an hour
than at 70 mph.
• Driving with the air conditioner on cuts gas mileage by about 2.5
miles per gallon.
• Experts say that driving smoothly—accelerating and slowing
down gently—can increase gas mileage by about 5%.

THE BOTTOM LINE
For Your Company
• It's possible to improve gas mileage by as much as 20% just by
driving smart. For a company owning 10 vehicles, that could mean
fuel savings of up to $1,600 a year.
• Switching to smaller cars or vans for fleet use lowers vehicle purchase and fuel costs.
For the Earth
• If all company vehicles improved their fuel economy by just one
mile per gallon, we'd save up to 80 million barrels of oil, enough to
drive a compact car around the Earth over 5 million times.

RESOURCE
• **Car Tips for Clean Air,** by Robert Sikorsky ($9.95), published
by Perigee Books. *Offers a wealth of gas-saving tips.*

A laser printer can use more than 10 times the energy of a daisy wheel or dot matrix printer.

17. GIVE GREEN GIFTS

*For the cost of Neiman Marcus' cheapest executive
desk set, you can plant 500 trees.*

Nearly every company gives gifts—to employees, customers
... even the mail carrier.

You know what they're like: trophies, baseball hats, paperweights, etc. You've probably got at least one of them yourself, gathering dust on a shelf in your office.

Why keep wasting money on throwaway gifts? Why not spend it in a way that benefits everyone?

GIVE TILL IT HELPS

• For the cost of a dozen fruit baskets, you could provide protection against poachers in an African wildlife refuge for a month.

• For the cost of a good pen set, you could adopt an acre of endangered land ... and pay for its maintenance and protection for a year.

• For the price of 110 golf shirts imprinted with your company's name, Adopt-a-Stream could buy an aquarium for a school to raise salmon eggs ... which could then be released into a river.

SIMPLE THINGS TO DO

• If your company already gives gifts on a regular basis, find out if management is willing to substitute comparable items that can benefit the environment.

• This isn't limited to making donations to environmental causes. You can still give gifts. For example, instead of a pen set or desk accessory, why not give a desktop recycling container or a battery recharger? Gardener's Supply offers a Panama hat made in the rainforests of Guatemala. And a San Francisco company called Used Rubber USA manufactures high fashion jewelry and handbags out of old tires.

• Consider giving copies of this or other environmental books. Or make a donation in customers' or employees' names to an environmental organization or a rainforest preservation project.

Patagonia donates 10% of its pretax profits to

For Your Company

• You'll be making a statement that your company is concerned about the environment.

For the Earth

• Whatever issue you choose to invest in—recycling, the rainforest, wildlife preservation, etc.—your money will make a difference.

• Bonus: Environmentally responsible gifts set an example for other companies, and help make everyone aware of environmental issues.

RESOURCES

• **The Basic Foundation,** P.O. Box 47012, St. Petersburg, FL 33743. (813) 526-9562. *Buy a tree or an acre of forest in an endangered Costa Rican forest.*

• **Co-Op America,** 2100 M St. NW, Washington, DC 20036. (202) 223-1881.

• **The Daily Planet,** P.O. Box 1313, New York, NY 10013. (212) 334-0006.

• **Earth Care Paper Inc.,** P.O. Box 7070, Madison, WI 53707. (608) 277-2900.

• **Greenpeace,** P.O. Box 77048, San Francisco, CA 94107. (800) 456-4029.

• **The Nature Company,** P.O. Box 2310, Berkeley, CA 94702. (800) 227-1114.

• **The Nature Conservancy,** 1815 N Lynn St., Arlington, VA 22209. (703) 841-2907.

• **Real Goods,** 966 Mazzoni St., Ukiah, CA 95482. (800) 762-7325.

• **Seventh Generation,** Colchester, VT 05446. (800) 456-1177.

• **Used Rubber USA**, 597 Haight St., San Francisco, CA 94117. (415)-626-7855.

• **Gardener's Supply**, 128 Intervale Rd., Burlington, VT 05401.

support the efforts of over 250 environmental organizations.

18. DON'T BE A DRIP

U.S. office workers use enough water every day to fill 17,500 Olympic-sized swimming pools.

That faucet in the restroom has been leaking for over a year, but no one ever seems to do anything about it. Well, who cares? It's only one little leak.

But that "little leak" may be costing your company a lot of money— as well as wasting water.

And the fact is, faucets can waste water even when they're not leaking. According to some water utilities, the average faucet puts out as much as 3-5 gallons of water per minute—much more than anyone needs. There are simple solutions: Maintenance and a device called a "low-flow aerator."

LIQUID ASSETS

• A leaky faucet that fills a coffee cup in 10 minutes will waste an estimated 3,000 gallons of water a year.

• Depending on water pressure, it's easy to use several gallons of water just washing your hands and face.

• But by installing a simple device called a low-flow aerator, you can cut the water flow by 25-50% without feeling the difference.

• The reason: Air is mixed into the flow, so it seem like there's more water than there really is.

• Faucet aerators save energy, too, by cutting hot water waste.

SIMPLE THINGS TO DO
Check Your Faucets

• Conduct a water audit and find out which faucets are leaking and /or need low-flow aerators.

• Your maintenance department may be able to help. Or you can organize people on every floor to do the survey.

According to *The Solution to Pollution in the Workplace,*

Cut the Flow

• Report leaks to the building engineer or landlord. In many cases, all it takes to repair a faucet is a new washer or tightening a fitting.

• Put low-flow aerators on all faucets that need them. They cost a few dollars each and can be installed in a few minutes.

• Do people often leave the water running? Consider installing spring-loaded valves or automatic sensors to shut faucets off automatically.

• If you're installing new equipment, ask your plumbing contractor to look into low-flow faucets.

SUCCESS STORY

• The Rockledge Towers office building in Boston installed 590 faucet aerators at a cost of $4,720. The aerators save the building owners 4.2 million gallons of water a year. The investment paid for itself within three months in water and energy savings and will continue to save over $18,000 a year in water costs.

THE BOTTOM LINE

For Your Company

• According to one source, a 100-employee company uses an average of 40,000 gallons of water each year from its faucets alone. So by installing low-flow aerators, that business could save up to 10,000 gallons of water annually—enough to pay for the investment in under a year.

For the Earth

• If only 10,000 businesses with 100 employees—or the equivalent—installed low-flow faucet aerators, America could save 100 million gallons of water a year.

RESOURCE

• **Perquod Associates, Inc.**, 129 South St., Boston, MA 02111. (617) 542-8567. *An engineering firm that will conduct water audits and recommend ways to save.*

over 1/2 of Americans live within six miles of where they work.

19. THE AMAZING FLUORESCENTS

*When the Environmental Protection Agency switched
to compact fluorescent bulbs, it cut electricity use,
costs and power plant pollution by 57%.*

Everyone knows about fluorescent lights—those long, flicker-ing tubes that give people headaches at work. Businesses have used them for many years because they give off a lot of light and use a relatively small amount of energy.

But here's something new: Lighting companies now manufacture fluorescent bulbs that look and act like standard incandescents. They screw into normal fixtures, give off a pleasant light, and come on instantly ... without flickering.

There's one way they're still different, though—they use only about a quarter of the energy of incandescents, and last about 10 times longer.

Have you seen the light?

FLUORESCENT FACTS

• It takes 13 incandescent bulbs to last the same 7,500 to 10,000 hours as an equivalent compact fluorescent.

• One benefit for businesses: You save maintenance costs.

• In addition to standard overhead lights, compact fluorescents are now available as reading lights, floodlights, spotlights and many others.

• However, they can't be used in all fixtures. They don't work with dimmer switches, for example. And they're too big for some stan-dard fixtures.

SIMPLE THINGS TO DO

• Check with a lighting consultant or contractor to find out which of your lighting needs can be handled by compact fluorescents.

• Let employees experiment with them to see where they work best.

Smith & Hawken deposits used fluorescent lamps with a recycler so

• There are new compact fluorescents being introduced all the time; ask contractors to keep you informed.

A SUCCESS STORY
• The Transamerica Pyramid in San Francisco replaced the 50-watt incandescent floodlights around the building's perimeter with 7.5-watt compact fluorescent bulbs. The total cost, including installing 450 new light fixtures was $14,000. The building now saves about $14,000 a year—$10,600 in reduced electricity use and $3,400 in labor costs saved by replacing light bulbs less frequently.

THE BOTTOM LINE
For Your Company
• The initial cost of a compact fluorescent is higher than you're used to paying—$15-$20 per bulb—but you'll save money in the long run. Over its lifetime, a compact fluorescent uses about $10 worth of electricity; during the same period, equivalent incandescents gobble about $45 worth of electricity. So you can save up to $35 per bulb—which is like earning 25%-50% interest on your investment.

For the Earth
• Substituting a compact fluorescent for a traditional bulb could, over the life of the bulb, eliminate the energy equivalent of about one barrel of oil or 700 pounds of coal, which would produce one ton of carbon dioxide (the major greenhouse gas) and 14 pounds of sulfur dioxide (which contributes to acid rain). By using fewer bulbs, you also cut waste.

RESOURCES
• **Green Lights,** *an innovative government program to help businesses cut lighting costs.* For information, contact the EPA, Global Change Division, 401 M St. SW, Washington, DC 20460. (202) 382-4992.
• **Rising Sun Enterprises,** P.O. Box 586, Snowmass, CO 81654. *Mail order company specializing in energy-saving light bulbs. Send $5 for their consumer guide/catalog.*

the mercury (a hazardous material) can be reclaimed.

20. TURN IT OFF

Inefficient use of office machines costs American businesses up to $4 billion worth of electricity every year.

I s your copier on right now? How about your computer and printer?

How much energy do you think they're using?

Here's surprising news: By turning office equipment off when you're not using it, you can save up to 90% of the energy it currently consumes. In a few years, that could be enough to pay for the equipment itself.

A SWITCH IN TIME

• Up to 70% of computers and related equipment are left on all the time—even though they're used infrequently.

• According to the Rocky Mountain Institute, you could save enough electricity by turning off a standard PC, monitor and printer nights and weekends to pay for the entire purchase price of the computer within a few years.

• Because of the heat needed to fuse images onto paper, laser printers and photocopiers are especially big energy users. Keeping them warmed up takes a lot of electricity, too.

• Some equipment uses much less energy than others. For example, ink jet printers use 99% less energy than laser printers while printing, and 87% less energy when standing by. Laptop computers use as little as 1% of the typical desktop PC.

SIMPLE THINGS TO DO
Computers

• Turn off computers if they won't be used for at least 15 minutes. It doesn't hurt hard drives to turn them on and off. Master-switched power strips will ensure that peripherals (printers, monitors, external drives) are turned off, too.

• At least, turn off the computer screen, even if only for a few minutes.

By developing a water-based ink to replace solvent-based ones used in its

• If a computer is left on just to take incoming transmissions, a device that turns the computer on when the phone rings may be worth looking into. The energy savings could pay its $200-$500 cost back in a few years.

• Use laptop or notebook computers instead of desktop models whenever possible.

Printers and Copiers

• Turn off printers and copiers when not in use. Some copiers have an energy-saving switch that puts the machine on "standby."

• If a big copier is seldom used, consider an inexpensive "cold fuser" desktop model that needs no warm-up. It will pay for itself by keeping the "hot fuser" copier off until it's needed for large copying jobs.

• Plug printers and copiers into a time switch to ensure that they're turned off after working hours. If you need the machine at night or on weekends, you can turn it back on by flicking a switch.

THE BOTTOM LINE

For Your Company

• Turning off just 10 PCs at night and on weekends could save $1,000 a year in energy costs—enough to buy another PC.

• Because most office machines generate heat while they're on, turning them off reduces the demand on the air conditioning system.

For the Earth

• According to the Rocky Mountain Institute, careful attention to efficiency and operation of office equipment could save enough energy during the 1990s to eliminate the need for nine power plants.

RESOURCES

• **"Electricity-Saving Office Equipment,"** published by the Rocky Mountain Institute, 1739 Snowmass Creek Rd., Snowmass, CO 81654. (303) 927-3128. *The report costs $950, but you can get a summary for $5.*

• **Cybex Corp.,** 2800H Bob Wallace Ave., Huntsville, AL 35805. (205) 534-0011. *The Phone Boot modem-activated power strip costs $3.75.*

wrapping papers, Cleo Wrap saves $35,000 a year in waste disposal costs.

21. START A "GREEN TEAM"

There is no ideal size for a Green Team.
It can be 30-40 people...or just 2.

All business projects need people to provide supervision and insure follow-through.

Your environmental projects are no different. If you're serious about your company's commitment to protecting the Earth, you'll need people in charge of the effort.

That's your "Green Team."

They're invaluable. If you're starting a recycling program, the green team can find the best company to pick up recyclables...and make sure the collection runs smoothly. If you want to switch to environmentally responsible packing materials, the green team can research and implement the change. If employees have questions about new eco-policies, the Green Team can act as a liaison between management and workers.

WHO'S ON THE TEAM?

• Volunteers are best. But some companies have successfully "drafted" Green Team members by assigning them the responsibility, and making it part of their job description.

• The most effective teams represent a cross-section of the company—different departments, levels and facilities. The goal is to make sure everyone in the company has access to at least one green team member.

• It's a good idea to include someone from the company's top management. This demonstrates the organization's commitment to achieving stated environmental goals, and guarantees that the group will have an advocate at high levels. Team members need to know they have a mandate to pursue eco-policies.

• Who's in charge? There's no rule. In some companies, the senior employee runs the group's meetings; in some, the chairperson is elected. And some groups have rotating leadership systems so each

The all-aluminum can was introduced in 1964. Now we use 80 billion of them annually.

member gets a crack at directing the group's efforts.

GETTING STARTED
• Once the members have been selected, an organizational meeting should be called.
• Pick a chairperson. If there's no obvious choice, ask someone to volunteer.
• Set a few reasonable goals for what the company hopes to accomplish. The first order of business, for example, might be an environmental audit so priorities can be set. Or you may have already decided you want to start a recycling program.
• But don't be reluctant to start small with specific issues like replacing Styrofoam cups with ceramic mugs, or setting up a system for reducing paper waste when photocopying.
• The key to making the effort work is to be as specific as possible about what you hope to accomplish.

GOING PUBLIC
• When the Green Team is organized, the rest of the company should be involved.

• Note: Be ready for some complaints; not everyone will be sympathetic to your effort. In fact, a few people may actually be hostile to it.

• If you have the blessing of top management, think about arranging a company-wide meeting at which the Green Teams are introduced. Give people a chance to ask questions. Make sure employees know what's expected of them, and how they can use the Green Team to help accomplish environmental goals.

• Next best method to introduce the Team: Send a memo to all employees, followed up with a series of smaller meetings.

• Communication is the key to making your environmental efforts work—and the Green Team members are the communication links. If you're recycling, for example, and there aren't enough collection bins—or they aren't emptied often enough—employees must have a way to let management know; that's where the Green Team comes in

• The Green Team should give feedback to employees, too, with posters, newsletters, etc. How is the company doing? People want

The National Park Service has a pilot plastic recycling program.

to know they're making a difference. Are there tips one department can share with another? That's part of the job.

SUCCESS STORIES
• In 1990, Ace hardware Corporation formed a Green Team at its Oak Brook, Illinois headquarters. The group, which includes representatives from every department, meets monthly to discuss various corporate environmental projects. The team is responsible for implementing the company's recycling program, and works with manufacturers to help them address environmental concerns. Progress reports on meeting company goals are posted in the cafeteria.

• In 1991, the 1700-room Penta Hotel in New York City organized Green Teams for its 300 employees. Starting with a few leaders identified by the hotel's management, the group organized a half-day of festivities for employees and their families. The hotel organized exhibits, ordered samples and literature, and set up a kid's program. Everyone watched videos, played "eco-bingo," and won prizes.

By day's end, the group had formed Green Teams. Now team leaders meet monthly to discuss progress on the company's recycling goals and organize other activities. "If the information we provide trickles down to even 50 or 100 people," says Steve Leonard, the hotel's assistant sales manager, "I think we've been very successful."

THE BOTTOM LINE

For Your Company. A Green Team won't cost anything extra, but it will help you achieve your environmental goals. That will improve your business's image—inside and outside the company.

For the Earth. Anything you can do to successfully recycle, cut down on material use, improve efficiency, etc. is good for the planet.

It's estimated that over 1 million people suffer from a form of pesticide poisoning every year.

22. WRITE ON WHITE

White paper is worth twice as much as colored paper on the recycling market.

One of the hardest parts of making an office recycling program work is getting everyone to keep white and colored paper separate.

It's a pain to deal with, but most recycling services require it.

Here's a simple solution: Switch to all white paper. You'll save time, effort and even money.

DID YOU KNOW

• Most colored paper is bleached white before it's dyed.

• That means there are extra steps when colored paper is recycled. For example, more bleach is required to remove the inks and dyes.

• As a result, white paper is cheaper to reprocess—so it's worth more to recyclers. And they'll pay you more for it.

SIMPLE THINGS TO DO

• Switch to white paper for all your needs. Even legal pads are available in white. It may take a little time for some people to get used to the change, but it'll soon become routine.

• When the San Francisco law firm of Majestic, Parsons, Siebert and Hsue started an in-house recycling program, they agreed, reluctantly, to give up yellow legal pads and use white ones instead. "It's part of our commitment to recycling," says one of the partners.

THE BOTTOM LINE

For Your Company

• You can double the amount of money you make recycling paper by separating white paper from colored.

For the Earth

• Successful recycling programs save trees and other resources. If only 5% more office paper were recylced, we'd save enough to build a two-foot-high wall from New Orleans to Philadelphia.

23. FLUSHED WITH SUCCESS

American businesses flush more than a billion gallons of
fresh water down the toilet every working day.

M ost toilets use between five to seven gallons of water every time they're flushed. That accounts for as much as 70% of all the water used in some businesses.

But simple conservation devices and new types of toilets are available, and they cut up to 50% of the water used for each flush.

Saving water is good business. Take the plunge.

GETTING A HANDLE ON THE SITUATION

• If your toilet has a tank, a simple device called a toilet dam can save one gallon—or more—per flush.

• If your toilet has a lever instead of a visible tank (the tank is located behind the wall), a water-saving diaphragm can cut water use by about a gallon per flush.

• One leaky toilet can waste more than 50 gallons of water a day—that's 18,000 gallons a year.

SIMPLE THINGS TO DO

• **Conduct a "toilet audit"** to see which ones are leaking and which ones could benefit from water conservation devices.

• **Identify leaky toilets.** Put a few drops of food coloring in the toilet tank. Wait about 20 minutes (make sure no one uses the toilet during this period). If colored water escapes into the toilet bowl, you have a leak.

• **Install water-saving diaphragms.** All it takes is few minutes and a wrench.

• **Install toilet dams.** They're available at hardware stores for a few dollars … or make your own. Fill two half-gallon plastic jugs with water and put them in the tank. Caution: Don't interfere with the toilet mechanism.

Reynolds Metal Development Corp. cut its outdoor water bill in half through

• **Installing new toilets?** Low-flush models use as little as 1.6 gallons per flush.

A SUCCESS STORY
• The Phoenician Resort in Arizona installed toilet dams in 605 guest bathrooms. They made their own, using little plastic containers, at virtually no cost. They expect to save over 500,000 gallons of water a year. "We are concerned about water conservation as well as any savings we can generate," says Robert Stowe, assistant director of technical services.

THE BOTTOM LINE
For Your Company
• Saving water with each flush takes little effort and costs very little. In most cases, you'll see a payoff in less than 18 months. When the 52-story Rockledge Building in Boston retrofitted 580 toilets with water-saving devices at a cost of $12,760, it saved 2.6 million gallons and $11,740 on its annual water bill ... and paid for its investment in 13 months.

RESOURCE
• **Massachusetts Water Resources Authority**, 100 First Ave., Boston, MA 02129. (617) 242-SAVE. Offers a series of free water conservation bulletins for commercial buildings, hotels, schools, restaurants, and architects.

"xeriscaping," a technique that uses plants, grasses and trees that need little water.

IT TAKES

AN EFFORT

24. SET UP A RECYCLING PROGRAM

*Merrill Lynch recovers more then 20 tons of office paper
from 2,700 workers at the World Financial
Center in Manhattan every month.*

Your desk is piled high with paper again, and your waste basket is full. You can't fit one more "While You Were Out" message into it.

It's the same thing every day. You know you could be recycling all that paper, but you're not sure how.

Fortunately, recycling at work is so easy that you and your co-workers can do it without even putting in any overtime.

SIMPLE THINGS TO DO

Focus on Office Paper

• Offices usually start recycling programs with "white paper"—white stationery, photocopy paper, computer paper, any forms on white paper and white scratch pads. It's clean and has long fibers, so it brings the highest price when it's sold. That makes it worth your company's effort to recycle it, and worth a waste paper dealer's effort to pick it up from you.

• You need to know how much paper your office generates. The rule of thumb is .5 pounds per day for each employee. That's 2.5 pounds a week per person.

Find a Waste Paper Dealer to Pick Up Your Paper

• Ask your building manager for help. He or she may already be assisting other offices in your building with recycling programs

• Check with city hall. Many large California cities can assist you in setting up a system and in finding someone to take your paper.

• If neither of those approaches works, look in the Yellow Pages under "Waste Paper" or "Recycling."

• Be sure to ask: What materials will they take? How much will they pay for each material (white paper, computer paper, newspaper, etc.)? Will they sign a long-term (i.e. one year) contract? How often will they make pick-ups? Can they supply references?

• Does your company destroy confidential documents? That's important to know because recyclers usually can't accept shredded paper; it doesn't mix well with the rest of the paper.

• Most dealers won't agree to pick up anything less than 500 to 1,000 pounds, so you need to know how much waste paper you plan to recycle before contacting them.

• If you don't generate enough paper, talk to businesses in your building (or nearby) and see if they want to recycle, too. By joining together, you make it worthwhile for a collector to make a pick up.

• If you still can't get a collector, you can always drop off the materials yourself at a recycling center.

Who's Responsible?

• Recycling programs need attention to keep running smoothly, so it's a good idea to have a recycling committee—or a Green Team.

• Select one individual to act as a liaison among employees, management, janitorial staff and collectors who pick up your materials.

• Every division or floor (say, every 30 employees) should have a recycling coordinator. These people can answer questions and check to make sure people aren't putting trash in recycling bins.

THE SET-UP

• **The aim is simple:** You want to direct paper that's been going into a trash can into a recycling container instead.

• **Provide a small desktop container to each employee.** This can be a simple cardboard box, or a more elaborate container with separate compartments for different kinds of paper.

• **When the desktop box is filled:** Each employee empties it into a larger central container. This can be a barrel, bin or box.

• **Station one on each floor**, in hallways or near a photocopy machine. (A lot of paper is discarded there.)

• **Don't make employees walk more than 50 feet to empty desktop containers.** If it takes too much effort, they won't do it.

• **Keep it clean.** The success of your program will depend on making sure you get only what you want in the recycling bins. If they're contaminated with other material, the paper dealer won't accept it

So make sure the recycling bin doesn't look like a trash can. Label the bin; if you want only white paper, make sure it says so clearly.

• **When your bins are filled:** They're taken to a central storage / pick-up area. Office recycling programs work best when they're integrated with the trash disposal system. So in many offices, maintenance people simply transfer materials in the central bins to a storage area in the basement or at the loading dock.

• **Everyone needs to know about the recycling program.** Post a memo before you begin. Then invite everyone to a meeting. Show how the system will work. Explain what can and can't be recycled. A handout helps. Note: Let people know if it's a success.

• **Other materials.** You should also be able to find someone to pick up bottles, cans, newspapers or other materials if you have enough of them. Ask your paper collector if any other materials are accepted; if not, ask for a referral to a company that takes them..

THE BOTTOM LINE

• **It's good business.** Recycling programs can save thousands of dollars. The Boeing Corporation has actually saved millions.

• **It saves trees.** Since office paper is high quality, it gets used to make new paper...at the same time it saves money and landfill space. At Detroit Edison, all 1,800 office workers have desktop trays for collecting paper. Their program produces about eight tons of high-grade paper a week, and generates about $24,000 a year.

• **It saves resources...and money.** Chicago's 2,033-room Hyatt Regency hotel generates 7.2 million pounds of trash each month. To reduce this and its $200,000 annual disposal bill, the hotel started a recycling program in 1989. The equipment cost $25,000. In one month the hotel collects 25,000 pounds of cardboard, 20,000 pounds of glass, and 680 pounds of aluminum cans. The hotel's disposal bill dropped from $12,000 a month to $2,000.

FOR MORE INFORMATION

• *Your Office Paper Recycling Guide*, San Francisco Recycling Program, Room 271 City Hall, San Francisco, CA 94102. *A wonderful booklet; $5. Make checks out to City and County of S.F.*

• *Your Practical Guide to the Environmentally Responsible Office.* The Service Marketing Group, 8 S. Michigan Ave, Suite 2500, Chicago, IL 60603. (312) 332-0688. $7.95. *Recycling guide.*

In 1987, Americans earned over $100 million recycling corrugated boxes.

25. TAKE CREDIT

A 1991 Gallup Poll revealed that a majority of Americans could not name any company they felt was "environmentally conscious."

I f your company is doing good things for the Earth, why not tell the world about it ?

SHOW AND TELL

• Not all environmental claims are valid—and when people learn the truth, it can backfire on a company. One example: The controversy over biodegradable garbage bags.

• In the post-1990 Earth Day frenzy, companies haphazardly threw themselves into "green marketing." It seemed that overnight, every product became "good for the environment."

• As a result, consumers are skeptical and some businesses are reluctant to call attention to themselves—even though they're making honest efforts to protect the planet.

• However, a recent survey found that nearly 80% of Americans have changed their buying habits because of environmental concerns. So it's worth letting people know about your environmental practices.

SIMPLE THINGS TO DO

• Make sure you have all the facts about what your company is doing. That way you can build an "environmental image" based on the truth, not hype.

• Work with an environmental group. By asking for information and advice, you may find potential problems before they're made public. A responsible group will work with you in confidence.

• Avoid well-worn slogans and meaningless terms. Americans are suspicious of phrases like "environmentally friendly." Most people respond better to solid, believable messages.

• Work with all departments and top management before you begin tooting your own horn, so you're sure the message will be reinforced throughout the company.

At 3M, employees have developed 2,700 projects to reduce

Where to Tell Your Story

• Once you know what you want to tell the public, communicate it in a variety of ways. For instance: Your annual reports; product labels; advertisements; press releases; brochures; trade shows.

• Be ready to provide background material or relevant statistics to anyone who asks.

SUCCESS STORY

• When Arco introduced its low-emissions gasoline in California in 1990, it crafted an advertising campaign that received high marks for its rational approach. Arco recognized that as an oil company it would never be viewed as "green." But from an environmental perspective, Arco noted their new product was an improvement over what they'd offered previously.

THE BOTTOM LINE

For Your Company

• According to Jonathan Schorsch of the Council on Economic Priorities, "Consumers tell us that they have changed their purchasing habits because of companies' environmental performances. There is no question that companies that are doing the right thing have a competitive edge."

• Telling the world about your company's efforts on behalf of the environment is critical. How you back up your message is even more critical.

For the Earth

• By sharing your story in a positive, credible way, you set a good example for other companies to follow as you help to educate the public about how everyone can make a difference.

RESOURCE

Environmental Communication Associates, 1881 9th St., Boulder, CO 80302. (303) 444-1428. *An environmental marketing and public relations firm.*

pollution, saving the company over $500 million since 1976.

26. GIVE IT AWAY

*U.S. companies throw away enough desks and chairs
each year to furnish all the offices in Boston.*

Your whole department just got new desks. Now what are you going to do with the old ones?

Unfortunately, there's a good chance they'll wind up in landfills.

But they don't have to. There are lots of people who can put your old office equipment to good use. All it takes is a few simple phone calls to find them.

CIRCULAR FILES

• Each year American businesses buy about 3 million desks, 16.5 million chairs, 4.5 million tables, and 11 million file cabinets.

• Experts estimate that half this amount is discarded annually.

• Businesses also throw away millions of old or outdated machines, fixtures, supplies, computers, carpeting, books and vehicles.

• Much of this equipment is in working condition, but simply isn't needed any more. However, many companies throw away the items, because they have no system in place to distribute them.

SIMPLE THINGS TO DO

Keep Track of Surplus

• Have an employee group (your Green Team?) set up a system to handle unwanted equipment.

• Ask department heads to notify the group whenever there are usable items they don't want or need.

• Arrange for the items to be brought to a central storage area until they can be picked up.

• Don't overlook the little things. For example, old magazines can be donated to local schools, hospitals or senior citizen homes.

Pass It On

• Contact Goodwill Industries, the Salvation Army or other nonprofits. They'll usually arrange a pickup within a few days.

According to *Paper Sales* magazine, 80% of U.S. printers reported that

• Even better: Goodwill will set up "reuse bins" on your premises and pick them up when full. Bonus: Employees can discard clothing and other items from home in the bins.

• One organization will sell your surplus items and use the money to set up a scholarship in your company's name.

SUCCESS STORIES

• The Boeing Company has a surplus store from which nonprofit organizations can select items they need. In one case, Adopt-a-Stream selected $3,600 worth of surplus desks, chairs, computer stands and filing cabinets to set up an office. Boeing took a $3,600 tax deduction; Adopt-A-Stream now has the facilities to teach kids how to care for waterways.

• Boston area industries regularly donate unneeded materials such as Styrofoam, Mylar, fabric, wheels and obsolete computer and mechanical parts to the Boston Public Schools' Recycle Center, where they're available to teachers, children and parents for educational activities. In 1990, the center distributed over $590,000 in free materials.

THE BOTTOM LINE

For Your Company
• Your company can receive tax write-offs for donating things it might otherwise throw away.

• Donations can bring your company good publicity.

For the Earth
• If every company donated just one desk or chair it might have thrown away, we could save as much as 500 million cubic feet of landfill space every year.

RESOURCES
• **Educational Assistance Ltd.**, P.O. Box 3021, Glen Ellyn, IL 60138. (708) 690-0010. *They'll sell your donations and use the proceeds to establish a college scholarship for underprivileged youth.*
• **Gifts In Kind America**, 700 N Fairfax St., Ste. 300, Arlington, VA, 22314. (703) 836-2121. *They'll help match you to a donee and arrange free transportation through the American Trucking Association.*

recycled paper's performance was equal to or better than nonrecycled paper.

27. CORPORATE COMMUNICATION

American companies send an estimated 13.6 billion catalogs every year. That's enough paper to print over 7 billion copies of this book.

Communication is an intrinsic part of business. Through catalogs, brochures, packages, invoices, etc., your company is constantly in touch with customers and suppliers.

You send hundreds, thousands ... or even millions of messages every week. So why not take the opportunity to share your concerns about the environment, and pass along information that people can put to work for the earth.

HEAR, HEAR

• Company newsletters reach millions of people. One example: *Round-UPS*, an in-house publication of the United Parcel Service, is sent to 1.2 million customers and employees every quarter.

• U.S. telephone companies send out more than 130 million invoices every month—more than 1.5 billion a year.

• It's estimated that the average adult sees between 95 and 100 TV commercials a day, or about 12 days' worth of ads a year.

SIMPLE THINGS TO DO

For Employees

• Include eco-information in your company newsletter or other in-house publications. Print a regular column on the environment ... or encourage employees to write in and pass on tips.

• Arrange for speakers to visit during work or after hours to discuss the things employees can do. Environmental groups, utilities, and government agencies will often send speakers at no charge.

For Customers

• If you have a formal environmental policy, publish it in company brochures and reports.

At Walt Disney Co., employees are given awards for

- Include environmental tips in your company's catalog, brochure or billing statements.

- Sponsor a "community forum" on the environment. Invite speakers from environmental organizations to give presentations.

SUCCESS STORIES

- The Nature Company published an in-house 48-page booklet, *Stepping Lightly*, to allow its employees nationwide to share ways to help the environment at work. The booklet teaches how to recycle and gives tips on everything from wrapping packages to riding bikes to work. "It made them feel good about initiatives they had already taken," says Catherine Girardeau, communication coordinator. "And it got them fired up to do more."

- Earth Care Paper Company publishes a newsletter, *Recycle!*, which is inserted into all customer packages. The 20-page publication teaches environmental skills and provides resources for learning more and taking action.

THE BOTTOM LINE

For Your Company

- Letting employees know you're commited helps give them a sense of purpose, and adds value to the work they do for you. It can increase motivation, morale and productivity.

- Educating customers helps them appreciate your company and products.

For the Earth

- The more people who understand the environmental challenges we face—and what we can do about them—the better chance we have of overcoming them.

RESOURCES

- **50 Simple Things You Can Do to Save the Earth**, by The Earthworks Group. $5.95 postpaid from The Earthworks Group, 1400 Shattuck Ave. #25, Berkeley, CA 94709. (415) 841-5866.

- **The Green Consumer Letter**, 1526 Connecticut Ave. NW, Washington, DC 20036. (800) 955-GREEN. $27/year. *A monthly update on environmentally responsible products and services.*

recycling, carpooling, conserving water and planting trees.

28. WATT'S UP?

Lighting accounts for 25-50% of energy used in commercial spaces.

I t's past quitting time, and you're the last one to leave the office. As you walk out the door, you can't help but notice that nearly every overhead light is still on. Why hasn't anyone bothered to turn them off? Well, maybe the maintenance people will do it. Or will they?

BRIGHT THINKING

• According to NRDC, at least two-thirds of office lighting is wasted, either through inefficient bulbs, poor design, or improper maintenance.

• The main reason: Most light bulbs are inefficient. They give off more heat than light. With some types of bulbs, 90% of the electricity used is turned into heat, and only 10% becomes light. But many new bulbs cut energy use dramatically.

• Another reason: Companies don't plan their lighting needs when they design their buildings or offices. Modern design and architectural techniques can significantly reduce lighting costs.

SIMPLE THINGS TO DO

• **Do a lighting audit**; put light where it'll do the most good.

• **Use "occupancy sensors"** in rooms that are infrequently used—bathrooms, storage rooms, etc. The sensors detect people in a room. When the room is empty, lights are automatically switched off.

• **Replace regular spotlights** with reflectorized halogen bulbs, which provide a narrow beam, white light and 20-40% energy savings. Replace flood lights with reflectorized compact fluorescents, which cut energy use by 75%.

• **If you use fluorescent (tube) lights:** Switch to new T-8 trichromatic bulbs. They produce the same amount of light as standard "cool-white" bulbs, but have better color and use 20% less energy.

• **Install new electronic ballasts.** Each fixture has a ballast to regu-ate the current to fluorescent bulbs. The newer models use less elec-

Consider electric cars for vehicles that do strictly local driving. . .

tricity. Bonus: They don't hum or flicker like the older ones do. At about $25-30 each, they'll pay for themselves in as little as one year.

• **If you use mercury vapor lights:** Replace them with high-pressure sodium vapor bulbs. A 250-watt or 400-watt bulb produces more light, at lower cost, than the typical 1000-watt mercury bulb and is ideal for parking lots, loading docks and other outdoor areas.

SUCCESS STORY

• Southwire Corporation in Carrollton, GA, conducted a major overhaul of lighting needs for its 5-million-square-foot facility. They relocated lighting near work stations to increase efficiency, lowered some light fixtures to increase the amount of available light, installed sound and motion sensors in some bathrooms and storage areas, replaced incandescent bulbs with compact fluorescents, added reflectors to fluorescent fixtures and replaced mercury vapor lights with sodium vapor bulbs. Annual lighting costs have dropped by a whopping $180,000. Says Southwire's Jim Clarkson, "Energy conservation means eliminating waste to increase efficiency. It does not mean cutting back."

THE BOTTOM LINE

For Your Company

• Many lighting improvements can rapidly pay for themselves.

• Energy efficient lighting also can reduce air conditioning costs by 10% or more. For a 100,000-square-foot building, that could mean additional savings of as much as $2,400 a year.

For the Earth

• According to the EPA, if all businesses adopted commonly available high efficiency lighting techniques, we could save about 11% of all the electricity used in the U.S. We could also cut sulfur dioxide emissions by 7% and carbon dioxide emissions by 5%.

RESOURCE

• **Green Lights,** *an innovative government program to help businesses cut lighting costs. For information, contact the EPA, Global Change Division, 401 M St. SW, Washington, DC 20460. (202) 382-4992.*

At current rates, electric cars cost about three cents per mile to drive.

29. SHARE THE WEALTH

*Americans averaged about $115 billion a year
in charitable gifts during the 1980s.*

I f you're like most people, your mailbox is flooded with pleas for money from all kinds of groups ... and it's hard to decide who's worthy and who's not.

At millions of workplaces, the problem has been solved by something called "workplace campaigns." It's simple: Everyone gives a few dollars from each paycheck, and the money goes to a cross section of well-managed charities. It quickly adds up to hundreds of millions of dollars a year.

Why not use the same approach to protect our environment?

DID YOU KNOW

• Charitable donations are growing at an average rate of 10% a year. But environmental groups get less than 1% of that money.

• Workplace campaigns are the most cost-effective way to raise charitable donations. About 90 cents of every dollar goes directly to the charity. With direct mail campaigns, only 2% of letters get responses and only about 75 cents of each dollar winds up reaching the charity.

• Statistics show that people will give more if they do it in small amounts over time. It's easier to give $1 or $2 every pay period than write a single check for $25 or $50.

• There are now hundreds of workplace campaigns offering an environmental option. In most cases, employees can pick the groups that get their contributions.

SIMPLE THINGS TO DO

Set Up a Workplace Campaign for the Earth

• First, find out if there's enough interest. Talk with employees and management. Make sure everyone understands how the program works. Remember: It's strictly voluntary.

• If you've never had a workplace campaign, get help from experts.

• Most programs begin with a two-week campaigns to sign people up. Groups like Earth Share will set up a table at the entrance to the

U.S. companies release 2.4 billion pounds of pollutants into

lunchroom or in the lobby, answer questions, provide detailed information on each charity and pass out pledge cards.

• On the pledge cards, employees can authorize the payroll department to deduct a certain amount each pay period—or maybe just once—to donate. They can choose which charity the donation should go to, or have it sent to a general fund.

• The organizer will keep track of donations and provide information to be used at tax time. In some workplaces, companies also match some or all of the funds contributed by employees.

SUCCESS STORY

• In 1987, Apple Computer added an environmental choice to its annual giving campaign. It also added a local arts group and a medical research organization. The response was overwhelming. In one year, Apple employees more than doubled their donations .

• In 1990, Earth Share helped to raise $6 million from workplace campaigns from such companies as Tandem Computer, Sun Microsystems and many federal and state government offices.

THE BOTTOM LINE

For Your Company

• A workplace campaign involves some minimal costs—a few cents per donation for a typical workplace. But that money will be leveraged into a much larger sum and put to good use for the environment.

• Experts report that employee morale and motivation goes up during workplace campaigns.

For the Earth

• Thousands of environmental organizations provide valuable services in educating the public and mobilizing action to help the Earth. By helping employees to contribute to these groups, you make it easier for these groups to accomplish their missions.

RESOURCE

• **Earth Share**, 3007 Tilden St. NW, Suite 4L, Washington, DC 20008. (800) 875-3863. *They'll send you material about workplace campaigns and can handle all aspects of running it for you.*

the air every year. That's about 10 pounds for every citizen.

30. MAINTAIN A
GREEN FLEET

*A well-tuned company car can use as much as
10% less gas than a poorly tuned one.*

C ars and trucks aren't great for the environment, but it's hard to do business without them. In fact, American businesses put tens of millions of vehicles on the road every day.

The way your company maintains its "fleet"—whether it consists of 1,000 vehicles or just one—can make a difference to the planet.

PARTS OF THE PROBLEM

• More than 250 million tires and 65 million batteries are dumped into landfills every year. Old batteries can leak lead and sulfuric acid into groundwater supplies.

• Because few of the 9 million cars Americans junk each year are recycled, 10 billion tons of steel and other raw materials are wasted.

• Car air conditioners are responsible for 16% of ozone destruction. How? When air conditioners leak or are recharged, lost coolant releases ozone-depleting CFCs into the atmosphere.

• Used motor oil is a major source of water pollution. A single quart can pollute up to 250,000 gallons of drinking water.

SIMPLE THINGS TO DO

• **Computerize the maintenance schedules** for all company vehicles, and conduct regular tuneups. You'll improve gas mileage, lengthen engine life, and reduce the cost of running your vehicles.

• **Consider radial tires**, which improve gas mileage by up to 10%. And keep all tires properly inflated. Poorly inflated tires can cut gas mileage by up to 5%.

• **Avoid over-servicing vehicle air conditioners.** Servicing is usually unnecessary and discharges CFCs into the air. If an A/C unit needs repair, patronize shops with new devices that capture and recycle the CFCs. (Federal law requires most A/C technicians to have this equipment in place by 1992.)

Since 1971, Xerox has let employees leave for a year with paid salary to

• **Patronize repair shops that recycle** motor oil, tires, batteries and antifreeze and other fluids. Your company's dollars can be a persuasive force in getting service stations to become more environmentally sensitive.

• **Look into setting up recycling programs** if you run your own maintenance shop, contact your local government for information on how and where to dispose safely of car parts and fluids.

SUCCESS STORIES

• In 1991, General Motors began requiring its 10,000 dealers to recycle CFCs from car air conditioners. The company estimates that a dealer who services 35 air conditioners per week could recoup the cost of the recycling equipment in 23 weeks by not having to buy new coolant.

• To save gas, the state of New York stopped using full-size sedans in its fleets. The replacement: Subcompacts and small-sized wagons. Other conservation measures include buying re-refined motor oil, re-capped truck tires and re-manufactured auto parts.

THE BOTTOM LINE

For Your Company

• The costs of regular tuneups could be offset by the increased gas mileage your vehicles will get. In a year, you could save more than $100 for each vehicle driven 12,000 miles—just by keeping the engine tuned and tires properly inflated. Regular tuneups and other preventive maintenance also prolong vehicle life.

For the Earth

• If every company-owned vehicle improved its fuel efficiency by just 10%, we could save 370 million gallons of gas, and keep nearly 7.4 billion pounds of CO_2 from entering the atmosphere—as well as reducing emissions of many other pollutants.

RESOURCE

• **National Assoc. of Fleet Administrators,** 120 Wood Ave. S, Iselin, NJ 08830. (908) 494-8100. *Publishes an annual reference book ($35) with vehicle service recommendations, EPA gas mileage figures, other data and info on use of alternate fuels in fleet vehicles.*

work for nonprofit groups, including many environmental organizations.

31. LEAF IT ALONE

Imagine 400 25-pound trash bags bulging with grass clippings. That's what just one acre of lawn yields in a year.

American businesses are always looking for ways to eliminate waste and cut costs.

Here's a good one: Start composting instead of paying someone to haul your landscape waste to an overflowing landfill.

A YARD AND A HALF

• U.S. companies landfill 6 million tons of yard waste every year. That's about 4% of our annual trash.

• In landfills, yard waste doesn't get the sunlight or oxygen it needs to decompose easily. In fact, it releases methane gas, which can pollute groundwater, and contributes to global warming.

• But if it's left to decompose naturally, yard waste adds nutrients such as nitrogen, potassium and phosphorous to the soil.

SIMPLE THINGS TO DO

Start Composting

• **Ask your company's landscaping service** what they know about composting. Do they have the equipment needed to shred leaves and chip branches? Are they willing to learn?

• **Consider setting up your own composting system.** You need a small outside area and some equipment (See Resources).

• **Let someone else do it.** Some companies will compost your waste and sell it to gardeners.

• **Call your state or local solid waste office** to see if it operates a municipal composting program.

Rake Expectations

• **Let It Lie.** Keep grass 2-3 inches high, and trim it a little at a time. Clippings will drop between the blades. They'll help the soil retain moisture, prevent weeds, and fertilize the soil.

To take polluting cars off the roads, Ford and Unocal bought

• Several manufacturers sell mowers with blades that chop clippings into fine particles and blow them down into the grass roots.

SUCCESS STORIES

• The Greater Cleveland Ecological Association composts 250,000 cubic yards of leaves a year, turning it into 20,000 cubic yards of compost; only 3% of residues goes into landfills. It sells the compost for $200,000, enough to finance the operation.

• Gardener's Supply and the city of Burlington, VT, formed a partnership to turn yard waste into compost. Businesses and residents who drop off 1 to 20 bags of leaves get a corresponding amount of compost in return. Gardener's Supply came out ahead; because of their efforts, they immediately increased their customer base.

THE BOTTOM LINE

For Your Company

• While each landscaped area is unique, the waste from a typical acre of trees and grass, if recycled instead of dumped, could save $80 a year in trash hauling fees and $400 a year in reduced costs for fertilizer and mulch.

For the Earth

• By reducing yard trash, we can save dwindling landfill space. For example: In Florida, 16 million tons of solid waste is generated annually; experts estimate that nearly one-quarter of it could easily be composted or used for mulch.

RESOURCES

• **Gardener's Supply,** 128 Intervale Rd., Burlington, VT 05401. (802) 863-1700. *A good source for products and information.*

• **Biocycle: The Journal of Waste Recycling.** JG Press, Inc. P.O. Box 351, Emmaus, PA 18049. (215) 967-4135. *A monthly magazine that covers waste reduction and composting. $55 per year.*

• **BioActivator,** *a powder that activates and speeds up composting.* $9.95 postpaid from Necessary Trading Co., New Castle, VA 24127. (703) 864-5103.

1,000 pre-1971 cars from Southern Californians for $700 each.

32. EVERYONE INTO THE POOL

*Commuters waste enough gasoline in traffic jams every year
to drive a car to the sun and back more than 300 times.*

I f you're concerned about the effect of cars on the environment but
can't take public transportation, here's an alternative: Join a carpool or a vanpool.... And get your business to support it.

DID YOU KNOW
• Bumper-to-bumper traffic wastes an estimated 3 billion gallons of
gasoline a year—5% of the nation's annual gas consumption.

• A University of California study found that people who drive in
congested traffic have increased blood pressure.

• According to surveys, the main reasons people don't carpool are:
They want access to a car in case of family emergency or if they have
to work late; and they don't like the idea of riding with strangers.

• But ridesharing can actually be enjoyable. "Once most people try it,
they don't go back," says the manager of a Washington, D.C. area ridesharing program.

SIMPLE THINGS TO DO
Ridesharing
• Set up a ridesharing program in your company. The goal: Match
riders and drivers who live within a few miles of one another.

• One easy method: Place a large map on a bulletin board and have
employees pin their names and phone numbers to their neighborhoods
on the map.

• Make lists of the names and phone numbers of people who live near
each other and distribute them to each member of the group.

• Give employees an incentive by providing free or reduced-rate parking and prime parking spaces for ridesharers.

• If your company has too few employees to organize pools, contact

At United Airlines, food containers used for in-flight meals are recycled 30 to 40 times.

your local government or public library for the names of ridesharing networks in your area. Post and distribute that information.

Vanpools

• A company can also buy or rent vans for groups of employees to use. Employees can pay their own gas, maintenance and insurance. And instead of hiring a driver, let an employee ride at no charge and use the van on weekends.

• Paint your company name on the van and a message—"We're doing our part to reduce pollution." You'll have a moving billboard for your business's environmental commitment.

• Set up a "guaranteed ride home" program. Offer poolers free or reduced cost transportation home via taxis or rental cars if needed.

SUCCESS STORIES

• To encourage carpooling, a Seattle company provided a "taxi fund" for employees who needed to leave work unexpectedly or late. The company budgeted $8,000, but only $1,000 was used the first year.

• 3M, in St. Paul, Minnesota operates 112 vans carrying a total of 910 employees. Riders pay a monthly fee that covers all costs. Drivers pay a smaller amount or ride free and pay a per mile fee for personal use. 3M estimates the vans have taken 750 cars off the roads.

• When 20th Century Industries in Woodland Hills, CA, instituted a $30 a month parking charge for nonpoolers, 200 carpools formed almost overnight.

THE BOTTOM LINE
For Your Business

• Company-sponsored vanpools can pay for themselves. At 3M, all costs except administration are paid for by employees. The costs are reasonable: Employees pay only $57.20 a month for a 50-mile daily roundtrip.

• Vanpools can attract and keep employees who live at a distance, says a spokeswoman for Geico Insurance in Maryland. One of its vans drives 58 miles a day to West Virginia.

• Carpooling can build employee morale and productivity. 3M is

Commercial laundry machines set on warm rather than hot can cut energy use by 50%.

among the employers that have found that workers who rideshare are less likely to use sick leave (especially if they pay a flat monthly fee) and more likely to arrive on time and manage their time better during the day.

• In nine polluted metropolitan areas, new laws require employers of more than 100 people to take steps to increase carpooling beginning in 1992. If businesses voluntarily take steps now, "state governments will be less likely to promulgate more stringent requirements," says the Association for Commuter Transportation.

For the Earth

• The average commuting car holds just 1.8 passengers. According to Chris Calwell of the NRDC, if each commuting car carried just one more person, we could save more than 18 million gallons of gasoline and keep more than 360 million pounds of carbon dioxide out of the atmosphere—every day.

RESOURCES

• **Association for Commuter Transportation,** 808 17th St. NW, #200, Washington, DC 20006. (202) 659-0602. *Offers a bimonthly newsletter for employers and provides fact sheets on commuting.*

• **Check with your state or local government.**
Sixteen states have ridesharing programs; nine have special commuter lanes. Local programs can often be found in the phone book under "Rideshare."

Gillette's water-saving measures save over $2 million a year at its South Boston plant alone.

33. CLOSE THE LOOP

In 1989, there were 30 companies making 170 different recycled products. By 1991, 400 companies were making more than 2,400 different products.

E very week your office recycles its paper, glass and cans. It makes you feel good to know all that material is being saved.... But what happens to it after it leaves your business? That depends on you.

If there's a market for recycled products, each item you bring back will be used to make new merchandise.

Who can provide the market? Your company.

DID YOU KNOW

Paper isn't the only recycled product available. For example:

• Car and truck tires can be recycled by grinding them up and making them into rubber flooring—ideal for a warehouse, storage area or factory floor.

• You can buy pens, rulers, scissors and other office products made partly or entirely of recycled plastic.

• Garbage bags made of recycled material are available. And many recycling bins themselves are made out of recycled plastic.

• Recycled motor oil is readily available for cars or trucks.

SIMPLE THINGS TO DO

• Find out if any products you purchase are made from recycled materials. The best source for this information is *The Official Recycled Products Guide* (see Resources).

• Caution: Not all "recycled" products contain 100% recycled material. Some have only a small percentage. You may have to ask to find out the exact amount.

• Contact the manufacturer for a catalog or spec sheet. If there are several products to choose from, this information may help you determine which one has the highest percentage of recycled material.

Embassy Suites spent over $200,000 designing its Florida hotel to avoid

- Many companies will send a sample so you can decide for yourself whether the product will meet your standards.
- When you do purchase these products, tell others in your company. People enjoy knowing that they're contributing to saving the earth.

THE BOTTOM LINE

For Your Company

- Many recycled products are competitive, but some do cost more than unrecycled ones. However, higher costs are almost always the result of a weak market. When your business—and thousands like it—begin buying recycled goods on a regular basis, the prices will drop. Someone's got to be a leader. Why not you?

For the Earth

- Buying recycled goods saves energy and raw materials. For example: When a steel mill uses recycled scrap, it cuts related water pollution, air pollution and mining wastes by 70%. And recycling aluminum saves 95% of the energy used to make items from virgin material.

RESOURCES

- **The Official Recycled Products Guide,** P.O. Box 577, Ogdensburg, NY 13669. (800) 267-0707. *Single issue, $105; a year's subscription of three issues is $195.*
- **Carlisle Tire and Rubber,** Box 99, Carlisle, PA 17013. (800) 233-7165. *Manufacturers of Sofpave tiles—interlocking floor tiles made from recycled tires.*
- **PIMBYCO,** P.O. Box 240, Purdys, NY 10578. (914) 277-8872. *Wholesalers of pens, rulers, scissors and other office products made from recycled plastics.*
- **Rubbermaid Commercial Products,** 3124 Valley Ave., Winchester, VA 22601. (703) 665-8244. *Makes trash cans out of recycled plastic.*
- **Moore Oil,** 4033 W Custer, Milwaukee, WI 53209. (414) 462-3200. *They sell re-refined automotive, gear and hydraulic oil.*

beach lighting that would confuse sea turtles that nest on the nearby beach.

• **Acco International Inc.**, 770 S Acco Plaza, Wheeling, IL 60090. (800) 222-6462. *Makes three-ring binders out of recycled paperboard.*

• **Bags Again Inc.**, 1300 S El Camino Real, San Mateo, CA 94402. (415) 571-5511. *Manufactures plastic trash bags with 80%-100% recycled content.*

• **Envirosafe Products Inc.**, P.O. Box 1074, New York, NY 10156. (212) 529-3720. *Makes park benches out of 100% recycled plastic.*

• **Presto Products Co.**, P.O. Box 2399, Appleton, WI 54913. (414) 738-1349. *Makes Poly Stop parking lot bumpers out of recycled plastic.*

• **Enviromat**, 2286 Auburn St., Box 23, Hannibal, NY 13074. (315) 564-6126. *Manufactures entrance mats from recycled automobile tires.*

• **Asphalt Recovery Systems, Inc.**, 4415 W Montrose Ave., Ste. 1, Chicago, IL 60641. (312) 202-8308. *Manufactures a variety of recycled asphalt products.*

• **FSC Paper Co.**, 13101 S Pulaski Rd., Alsip, IL 60658. (708) 389-8520. *Makes adding machine tape out of 100% recycled paper.*

• **Niagara Fiberboard Inc.**, P.O. Box 828, Lockport, NY 14094. (716) 434-8881. *Manufactures various types of fiberboard from 100% recycled content.*

• **Recycled Products Inc.**, 54 S Brown St., Elizabethtown, PA 17022. (717) 367-0620. *Makes loose-fill cellulose insulation from old newspapers.*

• **Appleton Papers Inc.**, 825 E Wisconsin Ave., Appleton, WI 54912. (414) 749-8810. *Manufactures carbonless computer paper out of recycled paper.*

Eight of the 10 largest pulp and paper companies are headquartered in the U.S.

34. BEAT THE HEAT

According to the NRDC, it takes 3.6 billion gallons of
oil to heat American businesses every year.

Somewhere in your building, quietly (or not-so-quietly) working away, is a combination heater and air conditioner. The
engineers call it an HVAC system. It's a big, clunky device
that rarely gets any attention. As a result, systems are often poorly
maintained, or are operated incorrectly. In some cases, the equipment gets old and inefficient, and nobody even notices it.

If you're willing to take a little time, there's a lot of energy and
money to be saved.

Let's start with the heating system.

WHEN YOU'RE HOT, YOU'RE HOT

• Most building heating systems have two basic parts—the boiler
(which generates heat) and fans (which move the heat).

• You may be surprised to learn that the biggest energy user isn't
the boiler. It's the fans. They can make up as much as half of a
building's entire electric bill.

• Experts say that regular maintenance can increase equipment life
by up to 200%. On the other hand, ignoring maintenance can reduce equipment life by half.

• And an inefficient heating system can use twice as much energy
as an efficient one.

SIMPLE THINGS TO DO
Keep the System Tuned

• Have the entire heating system checked annually by a qualified
mechanical engineer. Don't leave this important task to your building engineer, who may not have the expertise to do the job right.

• Is the fan speed adequate for your building's needs? Ask the
engineer. If the fans aren't adjusted properly, the whole system runs
inefficiently. A simple adjustment may cut energy costs by 20% ...
or more.

• Clean filters regularly. You can tell the filters are dirty if there's dirt or soot around the ceiling vents. Dirty filters restrict air flow, requiring the system to work harder. Bonus: Cleaning filters also improves indoor air quality.

Upgrade the System

• Install variable speed fans. Most fans operate at a constant speed. Variable speed fans adjust themselves to deliver only the amount of air the building needs at any given moment. Installation costs are typically recouped within three years through reduced energy costs.

• If the system is over 25 years old, think about replacing the boiler. The cost of a new boiler can pay for itself in as little as one year through energy savings.

THE BOTTOM LINE

For Your Company

• Keeping a heating system maintained can cost very little, but can yield big savings in reduced energy costs. Experts say that most building owners can cut their heating bills by as much as half through preventive maintenance. For a 100,000-square-foot building, that's an estimated savings of over $7,000 a year.

For the Earth

• It's estimated that if just half of all workplaces used preventive maintenance techniques on their heating systems, we could save enough energy to heat *all* the homes in the United States for three weeks a year.

RESOURCES

• **American Society of Heating, Refrigeration and Air Conditioning Engineers**, 1791 Tullie Cir. NE, Atlanta, GA 30329. (404) 636-8400. *They'll help find a qualified mechanic.*

• **Energy & Economics—Strategies for Office Building Design**, available free from Northeast Utilities, Conservation and Load Management Dept., ECC Program Administrator, P.O. Box 270, Hartford, CT 06141. (203) 655-5000.

educating co-workers about office environmental policies.

35. COOL AID

*On an average summer day, American air conditioners provide
enough cold air to produce 16 trillion ice cubes.*

I f you work in a typical new office building, you can't open the
windows. That means when it gets hot and stuffy, your only option is to turn up the air conditioning.

Keeping things cool at work takes a lot of money and energy—
the equivalent of about 12 billion gallons of oil every year in the
U.S. alone. So it makes sense for your company to try to keep its
costs low, as well as the temperature. The best way to do that is to
make sure the air conditioning system is well-maintained.

COLD COMFORT

• An inefficient cooling system can use as much as 20% more energy than a well-tuned one.

• Most A/C systems use the refrigerant freon, which is an ozone-
destroying chlorofluorocarbon (CFC). When the system isn't properly maintained, CFCs can leak out—anywhere from an ounce a
month to a gallon a minute.

SIMPLE THINGS TO DO

Keep the System Tuned

• Have the air conditioning system checked annually by a qualified
mechanical engineer. Make sure that includes testing the refrigerant system for leaks.

• On larger systems, devices can be installed that will automatically
monitor for CFC leaks and other malfunctions. If something goes
wrong, it automatically notifies whoever's in charge.

• Ask your technician to use a device to capture freon during repair
and maintenance. These devices not only keep CFCs out of the atmosphere, they allow the gas to be recycled and reused.

Reduce the Heat

• Lights and machines create heat. By turning them off when they
aren't needed, you can reduce a building's cooling requirements by

Thanks to an environmental audit, Chevron USA was able to cut by at least 10%.

• Consider using shades and other window treatments that can keep heat out in the summer. (See page 84.)

Upgrade the System

• Consider installing a "variable air volume system"—a new, efficient type of air conditioner that controls room temperature by monitoring the amount of air introduced into the space.

• Want a less expensive device? Try a "variable air diffuser"—a ceiling vent that opens and closes according to room temperature. (It contains a thermostat.) It costs about $30,000 to outfit a 100,000-square-foot building. Energy savings could pay that back in as little as two years.

A SUCCESS STORY

• By installing a new type of A/C system that creates and stores ice during off-peak hours (when utility rates are lower), the 70-year-old, 9-story John Hancock Institute building in Boston cut its annual A/C costs by $25,000 a year, with no loss of comfort to employees. The system paid for itself in under a year.

THE BOTTOM LINE

For Your Company

• A small investment in air conditioning maintenance can yield a big payoff. A typical 100,000-square-foot building can save as much as $12,000 a year simply by keeping the system in good shape.

For the Earth

• If half of all business air conditioners were maintained at peak efficiency, we could save enough energy to drive a car around the equator an estimated 1.5 million times.

RESOURCE

• **Air Conditioning Contractors of America,** 1513 16th St. NW, Washington, DC 20036. (202) 483-9370. *They'll help locate a qualified contractor. Write for a free brochure, "CFCs and the Ozone Layer —What Air Conditioning Users Need to Know."*

90% its chromium and nickel discharges into San Francisco Bay.

36. CFC YOU LATER

According to the Natural Resources Defense Council, U.S. companies are increasing their use of ozone-destroying chemicals.

You've read about the depletion of the ozone layer ... and you're concerned. But what are you doing about it?

It's not easy to attack a problem you can't see.

The ozone layer is some six to 30 miles over our heads—high enough so most of us don't even know it's there. Yet 5% of it may already be gone due to human activity, and if the trend continues, all life on Earth will be threatened.

American businesses have a special responsibility to do their part to save the ozone layer.

FOUR ENEMIES OF THE OZONE LAYER

• You may know that chlorofluorocarbons (CFCs) are destroying the ozone layer. But do you know how your business uses them? The most common way: As a coolant (brand name, Freon) in air conditioners and refrigeration systems.

• Methyl Chloroform (also called *1,1,1 trichloroethane*) is weaker than CFCs, but is used in larger quantities. It's in products like correction fluid, dry cleaning sprays, leather cleaners and other aerosols—even some that say "ozone-friendly." Businesses use it mainly as a cleaning solvent in the fabrication of metal. It's also frequently used to fabricate adhesives and clean electronic parts.

• Carbon tetrachloride is a poisonous, nonflammable, colorless liquid typically used by chemical companies to make other chemicals.

• Halon, a potent enemy, is most often used in fire extinguishers.

SIMPLE THINGS TO DO
Do an "Ozone Audit"

• **Check manufacturing processes.** What are you using? Look for alternatives. Substitutes are available for many ozone depleters.

• **Air conditioners:** Have your building's cooling system checked for leaks.

Besides harming employees' health, tobacco smoke also makes

- **Refrigerators and freezers:** If you have a kitchen facility, have the refrigerator and freezer checked.

- **Fire extinguishers:** Buy only halon-free fire extinguishers. They say "Dry Chemical" or "Sodium Bicarbonate" on the label.

- **Cars and trucks:** Have the air conditioning checked.

SUCCESS STORY

- American technology helped create this problem... And the same technology can help control it. For instance, Whirlpool Corp. has developed a multi-layer, puncture-resistant recovery bag that prevents CFCs from escaping during repairs of refrigerators or freezers. It captures an average of 11 ounces of refrigerant per repair. By 1995, Whirlpool technology could keep up to a million pounds of CFCs out of the atmosphere.

THE BOTTOM LINE

For Your Company

- The same leaks that damage the ozone layer cost your company money. A properly functioning air conditioner, for example, requires less energy.

For the Earth

- For every CFC molecule that's prevented from entering the atmosphere, 100,000 molecules of the ozone layer may be spared.

RESOURCES

- **Alaskan Air Conditioning,** 1200 Chestnut Ave. N, Minneapolis, MN 55403. (612) 339-6851. *Manufactures new refrigerant for A/C and refrigerators that's 80% less ozone depleting.*

- **High Frequency Products,** P.O. Box 380016, Miami, FL 33238. (305) 899-8309. *Markets the Ozone Protector, a portable unit that recovers and recycles CFC-based refrigerants.*

- **Igloo Products,** 3499 Dabney Drive, Lexington, KY 40509. (606) 268-7546. *Manufactures CFC recycling equipment.*

- **Petroferm Inc.** 5400 First Coast Hwy., Fernandina Beach, FL 32024. (904) 261-6994. *Manufactures a CFC-free solvent for cleaning printed circuit boards and wiring assemblies.*

air conditioning systems work less efficiently and use more energy.

37. NO PANES, NO GAINS

Over 40% of the energy needed to cool a typical office is due to heat gain through the windows.

Your office window isn't just a sheet of glass—it's an energy system.
   It controls the flow of hot or cold air that comes into your office from outdoors.

If it traps heat inside during the winter, you'll be able to run the heating system less. But if it traps heat inside during the summer, you'll have to use more air conditioning.

A few relatively simple, inexpensive improvements to office windows can make a big difference in how much energy you use, how comfortable employees are, and how much your company spends on heating and cooling.

GLASS ACTS

• Sunlight coming through windows produces welcome heat. But in summer, that heat is unwanted. The air conditioning used to remove it each year consumes about 3% of the nation's electricity. One solution: Covering windows with shades.

• Windows need to be shaded in winter, too. Heat escaping through windows at night represents about 2.5% of total U.S. energy consumption.

SIMPLE THINGS TO DO

• **The easiest and cheapest solution:** Install reflective film over as many windows as possible. This can cut winter heat losses by 10-40% and screens out as much as 75% of the sun's rays—which cuts air conditioning needs.

• **Shades or blinds also reduce heating and cooling costs** considerably. But aluminum blinds are the least efficient.

• **If you're building or remodeling,** invest in double- or triple-

If your hot water heaters are located outside, paint them black. . .

paned windows. They can pay for themselves immediately; computer simulation programs can tell you whether you can buy a smaller (and less expensive) heating and air conditioning system as a result.

SUCCESS STORIES

• At the Pan Am Building in New York City, solar film installed on all windows resulted in energy savings of $9,000 a month. The investment paid for itself in under two years. Bonus: Most building occupants reported feeling more comfortable at work.

• The U.S. Federal Courthouse in Wichita, KS, replaced 665 windows with Heat Mirror glass, an insulating window. It achieved a 25% annual energy savings and in summer has cut operation of its air conditioning system in half.

THE BOTTOM LINE

For Your Company

• Windows are a key part of any building's energy system. While an investment in windows or shades can be substantial, many improvements yield a return on investment of at least 50% a year for five years or more.

• Investments can be enhanced by rebates offered by many utility companies. Southern California Edison, for example, pays customers $3 per square foot to install high-quality, efficient glass.

For the Earth

• According to the Solar Energy Research Institute, "Heat lost each year through windows alone adds up to the annual output of the Alaska pipeline." Making our windows more energy efficient will help reduce greenhouse gas emissions, cut air pollution, and fight acid rain.

RESOURCES

• **Marchant's,** P.O. Box 250508, Atlanta, VA 30325. (404) 355-6300. *Makes glass shading systems and solar screens.*

• **Southwall Technologies,** 1029 Corporation Way, Palo Alto, CA 94303. (415) 967-8713. *Makes heat mirror glass.*

• **3M,** 3M Center, St. Paul, MN 55101. (612) 733-1110. *Makes Scotchtint Reusable Sun Control Film and other energy-saving products.*

it will decrease hot water costs by up to 20%.

38. RECYCLE THE REST

About half of the trash an average company produces can be recycled.

I f you've already got a paper recycling system in place, you're probably ready to move on to other things.

It's a cinch to find more "trash" you can rescue from the dumpster—glass, plastic, aluminum, telephone books, corrugated cardboard…. There may even be recyclables that are unique to your business.

THE SECOND TIME AROUND

• Recycling your *Wall Street Journal* every day for a year can keep an estimated 13 pounds of air pollution out of the atmosphere.

• Recycled telephone books can be made into textbook covers, insulation, and record album covers.

• A recycled aluminum can is generally reprocessed and back on the shelf in less than six weeks.

• Glass never wears out. It can be recycled forever.

SIMPLE THINGS TO DO

• Make a list of the things your company uses that can be recycled.

• Check with your purchasing department. They may provide you with a list of the manufacturing or office supplies they buy each month. How many are being thrown out that could be recycled?

• Contact a waste exchange (see Turn Gunk Into Gold, p. 110.) or a local recycler to find out which of the items can be recycled.

• Find out how to prepare materials for recycling. For example, you may need to separate glass by color, crush metal cans or bag or tie newspapers.

• Recycle other material the way you recycle office paper. Select a recycler, collect the material and store it in a central location until it can be picked up.

• If you're only one of the tenants in a building, approach the management about getting everyone interested in recycling.

According to the Direct Marketing Association,

SUCCESS STORIES

• Recycling saves Chicago's 2,033-room Hyatt Regency Hotel $100,000 a year. Each employee is required to separate aluminum, glass, paper, and cardboard. Housekeepers have collection bins attached to housekeeping carts to sort material from the guest rooms. The company makes $20,000 a year just selling the recyclables.

• United Airlines recycles a ton of aluminum cans and eight tons of cardboard a week at O'Hare International Airport. The scrap earns $2,400 a month and saves $1,000 more in trash-hauling fees.

• Ben & Jerry's Homemade recycles 1,000 plastic pails a week. It used to cost $30,000 a year to send them to landfills. Now they spend only $6,500 to ship them to a recycler.

THE BOTTOM LINE

For Your Company

• According to some estimates, it can cost as much as $100 to pick up, transport and dump a ton of trash—and prices are going up. So recycling can save companies tens of thousands of dollars each year.

• Some recycled materials are valuable. For example: Certain plastics can bring as much as $600 a ton.

For the Earth

• The benefits of recycling are enormous. Two examples: Glass produced from recycled instead of raw material reduces related air pollution by 20% and water pollution by 50%; and recycling corrugated cardboard saves about 25% of the energy used to produce it.

RESOURCES

• Check the Yellow Pages (under *Recycling*) or contact your state recycling office to locate recyclers in your area.

• **The Recycler's Handbook,** $5.95 postpaid from The Earthworks Group, 1400 Shattuck Ave. #25, Berkeley, CA 94709. (415) 841-5866. *A comprehensive beginner's guide to recycling.*

most companies receive more "junk mail" than do residences.

39. A PALLET-ABLE CHOICE

It takes a tree ten years to grow enough lumber to manufacture one wooden pallet.

U nless you work in a shipping department, you probably never think about pallets. But every year, millions of them are dumped into landfills. Your company can't afford this needless waste ... and neither can the Earth.

GET A LOAD OF THIS
• Each year, U.S. businesses buy 500 million wooden pallets. Stacked on top of each other, they'd form a pile reaching 3,617 miles into the sky—the equivalent of 14,146 World Trade Center towers.
• 70% of those pallets are made from oak and other hardwoods. In fact, more hardwood goes into pallet production than into paper-making.
• Since the estimated cost to transport and dump one ton of trash is $180, U.S. companies could be spending up to $1.75 billion a year just to throw wooden pallets into landfills.

SIMPLE THINGS TO DO
If your pallets are only used a few times
• Buy pallets made from recycled corrugated cardboard. They're priced about the same as a wooden pallet, but they can be bundled with other cardboard and sold to a recycler.
• Cardboard pallets can support loads up to 6,000 pounds. But they weigh up to 77% less than wooden ones, lowering transportation costs.

If your pallets are used indefinitely
• Buy pallets made of recycled plastic. They cost 5 to 10 times more than wooden pallets, but can last *at least* 10 times longer. You can also repair them yourself. When they're no longer usable, they can be recycled and turned into other useful items.

Brooklyn Union Gas, Federal Express and United Parcel Service are three

If you use wooden pallets

• Use parts of damaged pallets to repair salvageable pallets.

• Buy a chipper to turn unusable pallets into wood chips, which are used as mulch.

SUCCESS STORIES

• A large industrial company (which asked not to be named) was discarding 36,000 wooden pallets a day after only one use. By switching to cardboard pallets, they expect to save $100,000 in disposal fees and make $40,000 reselling the used cardboard ... *every day.*

• Bell Labs in Whippany, NJ, used to fill two 30-yard containers with pallets every two weeks. They bought a chipper for $43,000 to turn the pallets into wood chips for use on their 190-acre property. The chipper paid for itself in a year by saving dumping costs and by completely eliminating their $7,000 per year mulch costs.

THE BOTTOM LINE

For Your Company

• Cardboard pallets cost between $6 and $7. They eliminate trash hauling fees, produce income from recycling and can cut shipping costs because they're lighter. Shipping a cardboard pallet holding one ton of goods costs about $12.50 less than with a wooden one. That's about twice the cost of the pallet itself.

• Plastic pallets cost between $35 and $55 and are designed to last for years. If they eliminate the need for 10 wooden pallets— as they should—they'll more than pay for themselves.

For the Earth

• Using pallets made from recycled and recyclable materials can save trees and significantly reduce dumping. Transporting lighter-weight pallets also saves on oil and creates less pollution.

RESOURCE

• **Gate Pallet Systems**, 350 S Campbell St., Valparaiso, IN 46384. (219) 464-0990. *Manufactures the Payload Pallet, made from recycled cardboard.*

companies that have converted some vehicles to operate on natural gas.

40. BUG OFF!

The average business uses 5-10 pounds of pesticides per acre on its lawns and shrubbery every year.

Y ou're walking up the sidewalk to work when you notice the smell of pesticides. Phew!…The gardener's been at it again. Of course, you appreciate the beauty of the landscaping, and the care it's being given. But isn't there some way your company can maintain it without using all those chemicals? As a matter of fact, there is. It's called Integrated Pest Management (IPM), and a growing number of businesses are discovering it.

DID YOU KNOW

• After broad-scale insecticide applications, a company's lawn may actually be *more* vulnerable to pest attacks.

• The reason: Insecticides also kill earthworms, which help keep turf healthy, and beneficial organisms that prey on harmful insects.

• Employees may not be safe, either. The EPA hasn't finished assessing the health effects of 32 of the 34 most widely used lawn care pesticides.

• Alarming news: six of the 32 are targeted for "special review" because they're suspected of causing cancer, birth defects or long-term illnesses.

SIMPLE THINGS TO DO

• Find people in your area who practice IPM. They'll start by assessing the condition of the soil—because you can't have healthy turf without healthy soil—and the types and number of pests present. They may use pesticides, but only in small amounts and only when absolutely necessary.

• They'll also use biological alternatives to chemicals. For example: Insect-attacking nematodes are used to kill white grubs, one of the most common lawn pests. And a naturally occurring bacteria can be used to control sod web worms in the caterpillar stage.

According to a Teague/Gallup poll, 60% of companies say that public concern about

SUCCESS STORIES

• The San Francisco Conservatory of Flowers switched to IPM to treat its 30,000-square-foot gardens after insect resistance made chemicals ineffective. IPM was more effective and cheaper to use. An added bonus: After switching to IPM, the Conservatory didn't have to close on "spray days," so admission receipts grew, too.

• After a large initial investment spent on redesigning its grounds to enhance drainage and air circulation, a 450-acre Florida golf course was able to save $30,000 in pesticide costs over five years by switching to IPM methods. The savings came from more targeted applications, use of biological and mechanical controls, and reductions in watering (which washes away pesticides).

THE BOTTOM LINE

For Your Company

• IPM techniques may involve higher up-front costs to monitor and design a program. But once in place, IPM is generally less expensive—and experts say it usually achieves a 90% or better reduction in harmful pests.

For the Earth

• Experts say IPM techniques can cut pesticide use by 80-90%. Because rain and snow flush chemicals into waterways, cutting pesticide use reduces water pollution and increases the safety of drinking water.

• Lawn-care pesticides may kill millions of songbirds and waterfowl every year. (They die from eating poisoned insects or from exposure to nerve toxins.) IPM can help save them.

RESOURCES

• **"Lawn Care Pesticides: Risks Remain Uncertain While Prohibited Safety Claims Continue,"** a free report from the General Accounting Office, P.O. Box 6015, Gaithersburg, MD 20877. (202) 275-6241.

• *Least-Toxic Lawn Management*, available for $8.50 from the Bio-Integral Resource Center, P.O. Box 7414, Berkeley, CA 94707. (415) 524-2567. *They also have a catalogue ($2) of publications on IPM and serve as an IPM information and referral source.*

the environment has made them switch to alternative packaging materials.

41. GREEN AUDIT

In 1989 Publishers Group West, a California book distributor saved $2,000 in energy costs by making a simple change in their lighting configuration—a trick they learned in an energy audit.

How can you get a clear picture of what your company needs to do to be more environmentally responsible?
Conduct a Green Audit.
Everyone knows what an audit is. But how does it apply to the environment?
A good audit will show you how to conserve water, save materials, and become more energy-efficient. That's good for your business ... and the planet.

IN THE AUDIT-TORIUM

• Green audits didn't even exist a few years ago. They were first created to help industrial companies determine whether they complied with federal and state environmental laws.

• Now they're used by all types of companies. According to Arthur D. Little Inc., environmental auditing is one of the fastest-growing areas of business consulting.

• It should be easy for any business to find an "environmental auditor." More than 100 companies now offer the auditing services. And there are hundreds of individual consultants.

• There are different kinds of audits; it depends on what your company needs. The most common audits cover trash, energy and water. But you could also do a transportation audit, a hazardous waste audit, a manufacturing audit, and even a product audit.

WHO'S GOING TO DO IT?

If You Do It Yourself

• It's less expensive .... and it's more efficient, because no one knows your company better than the people who work there. However, you may not have the time and expertise to gather all the necessary information.

• If you've set up a Green Team, it can play a key role by coordinating information from every department.

• Try to be as thorough as possible when gathering information. You can't make intelligent decisions without detailed data.

• Keep accurate records of your audit. You may need the information later to show to others. Be sure to date them; that way, you can make comparison audits in a year or two.

• A camera might come in handy to record your findings.

Go With a Pro
• It may be more expensive to hire an auditor, but professionals are probably quicker and may think of things you won't.

• Plus, experts have the experience to make recommendations on what to do next.

• Your Green Team can still play a role, acting as a liaison between the expert and the company.

• Another possibility: Contact your trash hauler, electric and gas utilities, and water utility company. They may conduct audits for you.

A DO-IT-YOURSELF AUDIT
• There are three parts to a Green Audit: planning, gathering information and recommendations.

• First, decide what you want to know. For example: How much does your company throw away ... and how much of it could be recycled? Or, how much energy does your company use, and how could it be used more efficiently?

• Next, create a plan to gather the information. Details will depend on the size of your business. If it's big enough, you could form teams to do the work; if small enough, you can do the work yourself.

• You might need an expert to review your plan.

WHAT TO DO NEXT
• When you've completed your audit, put all the information together into a single report, along with any recommendations.

• Circulate a rough draft among members of the Green Team and ask for their feedback.

• When you've compiled a final report, send a copy to the head of the company or the manager of your facility.

• Make copies available to employees.

SUCCESS STORY
• *Quad/Graphics*, a printing company in Pewaukee, WI, has conducted annual audits since 1987. As a result of the audits of printing and office operations and water and electricity use, *Quad/Graphics* cut ink waste from 942 drums in 1988 to 432 drums in 1990 by introducing new processes and by recovering and reusing ink wastes. Those changes alone save them $140,000 a year in reduced ink purchases and disposal fees. "They aren't big technical changes in most cases," says Leslie Ratay, communications manager. "It's a matter of introducing new processes, many of them just common sense way of doing things."

THE BOTTOM LINE
For Your Company
• Conducting a Green Audit requires an investment. Example: for a 400-person, 50,000 square foot manufacturing facility, a 4-5 day audit could run between $20,000 and $30,000. In most cases, the results reveal many ways your company can save money for years to come through more efficient use of resources.

For the Earth
• The potential benefits from Green Audits are incalculable, but there's no doubt that they're good for the planet.

RESOURCES
• **Environmental Communications Associates,** 1881 9th St., Boulder, CO 80302. (303) 444-1428.

• **Arthur D. Little Inc.,** Acorn Park, Cambridge, MA 02140. (617) 864-5770.

The paper industry is the third largest user of energy in the U.S.

FOR THE

COMMITTED

42. MAKE IT A MATTER OF POLICY

A 1990 survey found that only 15% of Americans believe that corporations are sufficiently concerned about the environment.

Your company has all kinds of policies—payroll and personnel, salary and sick leave....There are policies about jury duty ... and overtime ... and maternity leave ... and a dozen other things.

Now it's time to establish a policy to protect the environment.

HIDDEN AGENDA?

• First, find out whether your company has any written policies about the environment.

• If they do, let others know. Ask to have the policy posted or reprinted in the company newsletter.

ASSURANCE POLICY

• If none exists, ask management to consider adopting a policy. If they know employees are interested, they might be receptive.

• Offer to help draft a policy.

• Let anyone who's interested have a hand in writing it. Ask for suggestions. What are the important issues? What can different departments do to establish realistic guidelines?

• Organize informal discussions where people can share ideas and debate some of the issues.

• Build in flexibility. The policy doesn't have to be permanent. It can be amended as new technologies and laws emerge.

PASS IT AROUND

• Give everyone a chance to read the first draft and offer comments.

• Reprint or summarize the completed policy statement in your

Replace incandescent bulbs in "Exit" signs with

company publications, catalogs and annual report. Make sure it appears in employee handbooks and is given to new employees.

SUCCESS STORIES

• Employees at Tom's of Maine, which makes personal care products, put together a mission statement that commits the company "to be a profitable and successful company while acting in a socially and environmentally responsible manner." It was approved … and the company began using the policy as a framework for making all corporate decisions.

• Pacific Gas & Electric, the largest utility in America, now has an environmental policy that commits it to using efficiency improvements to meet 75% of the need for new power over the next decade. The rest it wants to buy from renewable resources, like wind and solar power.

THE BOTTOM LINE

For Your Company

• Polls show that your customers are looking for companies to do more to help the environment. They say they will change their buying habits to favor firms that are environmentally sensitive. Your policy represents your promise to employees, customers and the communities where you do business that you will do all you can to protect the Earth.

• It's obvious, but we have to say it in this book at least once: No Earth, no customers.

For the Earth

• Your commitment will help encourage others to take protecting the planet more seriously.

• However, it's not just your commitment, but the way you follow through that counts. The products you sell, the services you provide, and the way you conduct business all have an immediate impact on the earth.

9 watt compact fluorescents. You could save $21 a year per sign.

43. LET THE SUN SHINE IN

*Office buildings consume 30% of all
electricity used in the United States.*

People have been talking about the enormous potential of so-lar power for years. Many of the early predictions haven't been fulfilled yet, but in some areas, solar energy is already a reliable source of power. It's no longer science fiction—it's here.

RAYS OF HOPE

• According to the Solar Energy Industry Association, around 200,000 office buildings use solar hot water heaters (although most also use other energy sources as a backup for cloudy days).

• Some building techniques help capture the sun's rays—or block them—to heat and cool buildings. These are called "passive" solar because they don't require special equipment. They can cut heating and cooling costs by up to 30%.

• Sunlight can be harnessed to operate lights, signs and even electrical appliances like attic fans. This process of converting sunlight directly to electricity is called "photovoltaics."

• Solar calculators use photovoltaics. More than 2 million of them were sold in the U.S. in 1990.

SIMPLE THINGS TO DO

• **Investigate solar powered outdoor lighting.** Walkways and park-ing lots are prime candidates. The new designs charge automatically during the day to run efficient lights at night.

• **Set up a solar water heating system.** A 120-gallon tank costs about $3,000. It could pay for itself within six years in reduced ener-gy costs. However, this varies in different parts of the U.S.

• **Learn about other applications** where photovoltaics can provide electricity.

• **Building a new facility?** Ask your architect to incorporate

The Body Shop gives salespeople a half day off each week to

"passive" solar designs that make maximum use of sun and shade. Use windows to maximize light and minimize heating and cooling costs.

SUCCESS STORY
• Kleanerette, a laundromat in Santa Maria, California, installed 10 Radco solar panels to heat water for the 325 gallon tank it uses for its 50 washing machines. The annual energy savings was 40%. Based on energy savings and tax credits, the system paid for itself in under four years.

THE BOTTOM LINE
For Your Company
• While solar technology is still improving, there are opportunities to save money and energy with it now. You can start using solar at any level, from a $15 solar battery charger or calculator to a $250 solar-powered attic fan ... or a more expensive water heating system.

• Federal tax credits for installing solar energy devices still exist for businesses (but not homeowners). Businesses in California may be eligible for state tax credits, too.

For the Earth
• Every kilowatt of power generated by solar energy means burning that much less oil, coal or natural gas.

RESOURCES
• **Solar Energy Industries Association**, 777 N Capitol St., Suite 805, Washington, DC 20002. (202) 408-0660.

• **Sandia Design Assistance Center**, P.O. Box 5800, Albuquerque, NM 87185. (505) 248-2842. *An excellent source of information for how to build using solar techniques.*

• **The Solar Connection**, P.O. Box 1138, Morro Bay, CA 93443. (805) 772-8601. *They design and install solar systems.*

• **Real Goods Trading Co.**, 966 Mazzoni Rd., Ukiah, CA 95482. (800) 762-7325. *A mail order catalog with a fine selection of solar energy products.*

do volunteer work in the community.

44. WILDERNESS INCORPORATED

Collectively, American corporations own as much as a third of all private land in the United States.

We're not sure where the term *greenspace* came from, but it's one that businesses ought to know.

It refers to land—developed or not—that's used to support plants and wildlife. This can mean anything from planting a few trees near a warehouse to preserving a wetland.

Since American companies control so much property, they can have a huge impact by establishing greenspace wherever possible.

TREES, PLEASE

• Trees and other plants play a major role in cleaning the air and slowing down global warming. For example: A mature tree absorbs an average of 13 pounds of carbon dioxide each year.

• Researchers at the University of California found that the average temperature around cities and industrial areas can be as much as 9 degrees higher than in surrounding areas. The reason? "Heat islands"—buildings, streets, cars and other structures that soak up heat in the day and release it at night. Greenspace combats this problem; it can reduce energy bills in the summer by up to 15%.

• Industrial development and urban sprawl has already wiped out around 200 plant species in the U. S. since the 1700s. Another 253 will be extinct within five years if we don't do something about it.

SIMPLE THINGS TO DO

• Create as much greenspace as possible around your company's facilities. Look for parking lots, fields, abandoned facilities and other places that can be planted and developed.

• Start a botanical garden with unused land. The American Association of Botanical Gardens and Arboreta will help you. They offer a network of public garden professionals to share their resources.

Ben & Jerry's Homemade found a way to treat its own wastewater using

• Launch a company-wide (or facility-wide) campaign to turn an abandoned area into a park. Employees can raise funds and even do planting and construction themselves.

• If your company has unused or underused land, consider turning it into a refuge for wildlife, birds, or marine life. If appropriate, open the land to the public.

• If your company is developing land, try to compensate by preserving an equal—or greater—sized plot for wildlife.

SUCCESS STORIES

• Amoco Chemical Company's Cooper River Plant in South Carolina planned a wildlife enhancement program on 6,000 acres of land adjacent to a national park. The preserve will provide habitats for several thousand species.

• According to The Nature Conservancy, one company in Wisconsin worked with them to mitigate the loss of wetlands resulting from a new industrial park. To compensate for the 15-acre project, the company restored 425 acres on the Des Plaines River.

THE BOTTOM LINE

For Your Company

• It costs about $1,000 per acre per year to maintain traditional turf grass, exotics and seasonal flower beds—compared to $10 per acre to maintain a native landscape.

For the Earth

About 3,000 native plants are in danger of becoming extinct in North America. Greenspace gives them a home.

RESOURCES

• **The Nature Conservancy**, 1815 N Lynn St. Arlington, VA 22209. (703) 841-5300. *Works with companies to purchase land.*

• **Wildlife Habitat Enhancement Council**, 1010 Wayne Ave., Suite 1240, Silver Spring, MD 20910. (301) 588-8994. *This nonprofit group helps corporations improve their lands for wildlife.*

• **The Trust for Public Land**. 116 New Montgomery St., San Francisco, CA 94105. (415) 495-4014.

solar energy. It then is able to reuse some of the water.

45. WATER YOU DOING OUTSIDE?

The South Florida Water Administration predicts that at least 80% of U.S. businesses will be forced to ration water during the 1990s

I n 50 Simple Things You Can Do to Save the Earth, we talked about Xeriscaping—saving water by landscaping with drought resistant, native plants.

It's as just as important for businesses to xeriscape as it is for homeowners.

DID YOU KNOW

• If you water the lawn or landscape between 9 a.m. and 5 p.m. during warm months, up to 60% of the water is lost to evaporation.

• A type of grass called *Fescu* needs as little as 1/3 the water used by most common types of grass planted in the U.S.

• A running hose can waste 30 gallons of water in just 3 minutes.

SIMPLE THINGS TO DO
When Gardening...

• If your building has automatic landscaping sprinklers, talk with the people in charge of landscaping. Find out how often and at what times of day the sprinklers are used. Is the watering cycle modified after heavy rains?

• Water during the cooler parts of the day—before 10 a.m. and after 5 p.m.—to minimize evaporation.

• Ask your company's grounds maintenance crew to investigate water-saving practices. For example, using mulch on the ground around plants can reduce evaporation, requiring you to water less frequently.

• Investigate trickle or drip irrigation techniques that require less water to do the job.

A trigger nozzle on your hose will save at least 20 gallons when you wash your car.

• Look into "xeriscaping," a new kind of landscaping technique that uses drought-resistant plants and grasses that need far less water.

When Cleaning
• Review outdoor cleaning methods. Does the maintenance staff use hoses to clean walkways and parking lots? If so, this may be wasting water; a broom may be just as effective.

• Are cars washed on the premises? If so, find out whether hoses run all the time or are fitted with shut-off nozzles.

SUCCESS STORY
• When Valley Bank in Tucson, Arizona re-landscaped its property using xeriscaping techniques, replacing water-intensive grass with drought-resistant plants, it cut its water use and maintenance costs by nearly $20,000 a year.

THE BOTTOM LINE
For Your Company...
• Most water-saving techniques require little investment and can save money. Water is still a relatively cheap commodity—around $2 per 1,000 gallons nationwide—but the cost is rising in many areas. For some companies, the rising rates will mean thousands of dollars a year in increased costs.

For the Earth...
• Water supplies in some regions are becoming scarce. By cutting back on wasteful outdoor water use, companies can ensure that water supplies will be available for more vital needs.

RESOURCES
• **South Florida Water Management District**, P.O. Box 24680, W. Palm Beach, FL 33416. (407) 686-8800. *Write for a free color brochure on xeriscaping.*

Xeriscape comes from the Greek word *Xeros*, which means *dry*.

46. DON'T WASTE AWAY

Each year, U.S. industries generate roughly one ton of hazardous waste for every American citizen.

I s your business creating hazardous waste? It might be ... and you might not even know it. It's important to find out.

Unfortunately, you can't expect to eliminate all hazardous substances overnight—they're used in the production of everything from computers to videotapes to medications. But with the help of new methods and technologies, companies are beginning to cut down on the amount of toxics they generate—and much more waste reduction is possible.

CLEANING UP YOUR ACT

• According to federal law, even businesses that produce small quantities of hazardous waste—220 to 2,200 pounds a month— must send it to a regulated waste facility.

• But there's no totally "safe" way to dispose of these wastes. Even the best landfills might eventually leak.

• The General Accounting Office estimates that in 1990, industry spent $12 billion on managing toxic wastes. As more disposal sites close, pollution control regulations get tougher, and liabilities increase, the costs of dealing with hazardous material skyrocket.

• The best solution: Produce less waste in the first place. The Environmental Protection Agency estimates that one-third of all hazardous waste can be eliminated *before* it requires disposal.

SIMPLE THINGS TO DO
Identify the Problem

• **Conduct a waste audit:** Find out where toxics are being used or produced in your company; identify alternatives that can reduce total toxics output.

• **Need help?** Contact the Environmental Protection Agency or other sources like state programs, universities and consultants.

Of the almost 2 billion pounds of printing inks used,

Minimize Toxics

• **Redesign your products,** if feasible, so they require fewer toxic materials. For example, instead of designing a product that must be painted, use a base material that doesn't need painting.

• **Redesign the process:** Use less hazardous materials. For example, substitute a water-based ink for a metal-based one; clean metal surfaces with a mechanical abrasive instead of a chemical solvent.

• **Involve all employees.** According to a federal study, "Waste reduction succeeds when it is part of the everyday consciousness of all workers and managers involved with production, rather than just the job of those charged with complying with environmental regulations."

Recycle or Reuse Hazardous Materials

• You may be able to reuse some of your hazardous materials on site. Some companies extract and reuse precious metals, solvents or lubricants, for example.

• Contact a waste exchange to find out if you can sell or trade waste byproducts to other companies. (See "Turn Gunk into Gold," page 110.)

Dispose of Wastes Properly

• Separate hazardous waste early, before it gets mixed into other effluent. That makes it easier to target toxic material for appropriate treatment and to dispose of the nonhazardous portion.

• Investigate new technologies for separating or neutralizing hazardous wastes. Industrial scientists are experimenting with various electrochemical techniques to zap harmful compounds or feed them to chemical-eating microbes.

SUCCESS STORIES

• During a 15-year-period, the 3M Company cut its waste generation in half by using fewer toxics. For example, it reduced the amount of chemical solvents used to coat tape by substituting safer water-based or solid coating. 3M also recycles many substances.

about half will end up in the waste stream.

It's selling a byproduct of videotape making, ammonium sulfate, to fertilizer manufacturers, who convert it to plant food. Such changes have saved more than $500 million in disposal and pollution control costs. 3M sets pollution reduction goals, and in annual reviews it judges division executives and managers on how well they have met these targets, as well as their financial performance.

• When Eastside Plating, a Portland, Oregon electroplating company, substituted different agents for chemicals used in waste treatment, it decreased wastes by 50%. "We're cleaner, our people are happier, our productivity is up," says VP Jim Thibodeau.

THE BOTTOM LINE
For Your Company
• By taking better charge of toxics, your company can avoid fines, costly litigation, bad public relations and possible criminal suits against company officials.

• By reducing the amount of hazardous waste generated, you can save dramatically on transporting and disposing of waste, as well as new pollution control equipment.

• Waste reduction means lower worker exposure to toxics. That cuts health claims.

• "Waste reduction pays for itself relatively quickly, especially when compared to the time needed to comply with regulations, obtain regulatory permits, or site waste management facilities" says a congressional study.

For the Earth
• Improper disposal of hazardous waste often pollutes groundwater—the source of drinking water for more than 50% of Americans. Reducing hazardous waste will mean a safer water supply.

RESOURCE
• **Environmental Protection Agency,** Pollution Prevention Information Clearinghouse (PPIC), 8400 Westpark Dr., McLean, VA 22102. (703) 821-4800.

Esprit de Corp was the first major retailer to print its catalogs on recycled paper.

47. A GREEN BLUEPRINT

We spend $12 billion a year on formaldehyde-emitting wood products such as plywood and particle board.

P lanning a new building? Remodeling your office? You're probably more concerned with how much it'll cost than anything else. But your choice of building materials and the way you dispose of construction wastes are important, too.

A growing number of builders and designers are concerned with how their work affects the environment—from siting to design to the waste systems they install.

If you're not involved in the designing and construction process in your company, why not pass this along to the people who are?

DID YOU KNOW

• Many types of plywood and particle board emit formaldehyde, a known carcinogen.

• Construction affects the rainforests. Much of the rainforest wood imported into the U.S. arrives in the form of plywood and paneling. It's often used in new buildings.

• Foam insulation used on roofs and pipes may contain ozone-depleting CFCs.

• Loose soil from construction sites is a major contributor to "run-off" pollution in streams and rivers.

SIMPLE THINGS TO DO

When planning sites and landscaping

• Take maximum advantage of sunlight for lighting and passive solar heating.

• Plant deciduous trees on the south side to provide summer shade; also shade roofs, air conditioning coils and windows. As few as three trees around a small office building can cut cooling bills by 10-50%, according to the American Forestry Association.

When selecting materials

• Consult the American Institute of Architects for advice on choosing materials that do the least harm in their harvesting or mining, use and disposal.

• Try to use recycled materials.

• Use materials that do not require toxic protective coatings or treatments.

• Avoid oil-based paints and try to find substitutes for vinyl floor and wall coverings, particle boards, and certain types of carpets, which can all emit dangerous chemicals.

• Try to limit purchases to "certified" woods from suppliers practicing sustainable rainforest management.

During construction

• Protect trees and other vegetation. Be sure the whole crew is alerted to tree-saving steps like avoiding soil compaction over (and excavation near) roots.

• Reduce soil runoff into streams or waterways by retaining as much ground cover as possible. Erect barriers at the edge of the site to trap runaway soils.

• Consider donating surplus building materials to an organization that builds housing for low-income or homeless people. Don't throw it away.

A SUCCESS STORY

• When the Environmental Defense Fund renovated a 15,000-square-foot office in New York, it chose a location with windows that could be opened, and developed a ventilation system that exceeded federal requirements for circulating air. They also bought particle board without formaldehyde, used natural materials like solid woods that didn't emit gases, and tacked down the carpeting instead of using glue. The cost: $40 per square foot, low for New York. Everyone appreciated it: "They feel an attempt was made to create a space for them as human beings," says administration director Paul Wycisk.

At its Chicago hub, United Airlines recycles a ton of aluminum cans a week from its flights.

THE BOTTOM LINE

For Your Company

• "Absenteeism is lower and productivity higher in cleaner buildings," says environmental architect William McDonough.

• Environmentally sensitive buildings do not necessarily cost more to build. And they can offer savings over conventional buildings when long-term energy savings are factored in.

For the Earth

• Adopting different design approaches and building materials will "help reduce global warming, ozone depletion, energy consumption, air and water pollution and solid waste," the AIA says.

• Billions of dollars are spent each year on construction and interior design materials. If more businesses change their purchasing habits, suppliers will have a stronger incentive to shift to environmentally sensitive materials.

RESOURCES

• **American Institute of Architects** (AIA), 1735 New York Ave., NW, Washington, DC 20006. (202) 626-7300. *Developing an "Environmental Resource Guide" for architects and other interested parties on environmentally sensitive materials, methods and energy considerations. Contact them for cost.*

• **Rainforest Alliance**, 270 Lafayette St., Suite 512, New York, NY 10012. (212) 941-1900. *Write for a free brochure: "First Cut: A Primer on Tropical Wood Use and Conservation."*

General Electric tracks where its paper goes after it has been recycled . . . and then buys it back.

48. TURN GUNK INTO GOLD

Natural Products Corp. in Shippersburg, PA, turns wood chips discarded by a furniture maker into birdhouse kits and fuel.

G ot any brewery sludge, used industrial lubricants, or plastic diaper trimmings around? Would you believe there are companies that would love to have them?

It's true. Increasingly, manufacturers are finding uses for waste products from other industries.

How do you find a company to work with? "Waste exchanges."

If anyone can help you, they can.

WASTING AWAY

• U.S. industry produces nearly 11 billion tons of scrap paper, wood, plastic and other nonhazardous waste each year. They also produce 275 million tons of toxics. Only a small fraction of this waste is recycled.

• These discards can be reused in surprising ways. For example: Plastic waste can be molded into park benches; diaper tape can become coat hangers; shredded paper can be turned into home insulation; old tires become tugboat bumpers and asphalt.

• About two dozen North American "waste exchanges" help connect buyers and sellers. What are they? "Think of us as a dating service, matching waste generators with waste recyclers," suggests Lewis Cutler, of the Northeast Industrial Waste Exchange in Syracuse, N.Y.

SIMPLE THINGS TO DO

Contact a waste exchange

• Some are branches of state governments; others are run by universities or by independent nonprofit groups.

• They publish catalogs or provide computerized listings of substances for sale or materials wanted. Some charge a fee for ads, others are free.

• Try running an ad in a trade publication. "A lot of companies don't realize their waste is recyclable; sometimes an ad is the only way to find

Environmental Resource Return Corp. in Portsmouth, NH, recycles up to

out," says one waste exchange manager.

Work out the details

• Everything's negotiable, from the purchase price to transportation of the waste.

• **But take note:** If you're selling hazardous waste, your company is liable if it's disposed of improperly by the buyer. For your protection, "Know who you're doing business with and exactly what they intend to do with your waste," counsels one expert.

SUCCESS STORY

• A Georgia Pacific pulp mill in Bellingham, Washington treats its acidic wastewater with alkaline lime waste generated by three makers of welding gas. The gas companies are happy to save landfill fees, so they charge GP nothing for the lime. GP pays $20 a ton to transport it, but still saves $65 a ton over the cost of new lime. "It takes some quarterbacking" to make the arrangements, says purchasing manager Robert Ellerby, "but it's good for everyone—and the environment."

THE BOTTOM LINE

For Your Company

• Waste disposal costs are mounting as landfills fill up. Nonhazardous material disposal averages $27 per ton; hazardous material disposal can cost as much as $2,000 a ton. For many companies, it's now cheaper to recycle waste than to dump it.

For the Earth

• Recycling prevents pollution by reducing the amount of waste discarded in landfills, burned in incinerators, treated in sewage plants, or dumped illegally. It also makes the most of resources we already have.

RESOURCE

• **Northeast Industrial Waste Exchange,** 90 Presidential Plaza, Suite 122, Syracuse, NY 13202. (315) 422-6572. *They'll locate the waste exchange closest to your company.*

500 tons of building rubble, asphalt and concrete every day.

49. OLD WATER INTO NEW

American industry uses 28 billion gallons of fresh water every day. That's enough to fill a glass tank one mile long, one mile wide and 50 yards high.

Water is crucial to thousands of industries. You can't walk through an automotive plant, a textile mill or a food processing company without seeing rivers of it flowing through the manufacturing process.

In the past, the easiest thing for a company to do was dump dirty water into local sewers and let treatment plants deal with it. But laws are getting tougher, and water is getting scarce and expensive. Many companies are finding it pays to recycle their water.

This isn't a project for an average office worker—it's a capital-intensive, highly specialized operation. But it's an important one for businesses to tackle, and that's why we've included it here.

DID YOU KNOW

• Every day, more than 28 billion gallons of water are used for industrial purposes. That's more than 7 trillion gallons a year.

• That water costs companies about $14 billion a year.

• It takes 24 gallons of water to make one pound of plastic, 55 gallons to make one pound of synthetic rubber, 101 gallons to make a pound of cotton, 518 gallons to make one automobile tire, 1,500 gallons to process a barrel of beer and 35,500 gallons to produce one automobile.

• Some industrial wastewater contains toxic chemicals like benzene or chlorine, which aren't completely filtered out at wastewater plants. The result: These chemicals can get into rivers, or even back into our drinking water. But this water *can* be reused for manufacturing purposes.

SIMPLE THINGS TO DO

• **Do a wastewater audit.** Ask how much water is being

Painting the outside of your building a light color will

discharged and what it contains.

• **Find a consultant.** Since every system is unique, you need someone who's knowledgeable about your industrial process.

• **Check with your company's trade association.** Someone might've already done your research for you.

SUCCESS STORIES

• Polaroid Corp. devised a way to reuse wastewater that was being sent out for disposal at a cost of $2 a gallon. Adding some piping and a holding tank, they cut water use by 80% and save at least $30,000 a year.

• The Gillette Company cut the amount of water used to make razor blades from 730 million gallons to 156 million gallons a year. A water recirculation system was an important part of this conservation program. Says Cameron D. Beers, director of administrative services: "We weren't reinventing the wheel, but sharing solutions." Companywide, Gillette now saves about $1.5 million annually in its water and sewage bills.

THE BOTTOM LINE

For Your Company

• Recycling water can cut water use by 25% to 70%. In addition, it reduces the possibility of discharging contaminated waste.

For the Earth

• Less than 1% of the earth's surface is made up of liquid freshwater. We may not be in danger of running out of water, but we are short on water that's clean enough to drink and close enough to use.

RESOURCES

• **Water and WasteWater Equipment Manufacturing Association,** 101 E. Holly Ave. Ste. 14, Sterling, VA 22170. (703) 444-1777. *Its members are manufacturers of water or wastewater equipment.*

• **Resource Management Associates Inc.,** P.O. Box 251, West Barnstable, MA 02688. *Consults on wastewater treatment options.*

reflect the sun's rays, reducing air conditioning bills.

50. SPREAD THE WORD

I f you've made it through this book, you've already invested time and energy in changing the way you do business.

Here's something else you can do: Spread the word; let other business people know there are things they can do right now to help protect the environment.

There is no question that the 1990s are a critical point in human history. We can make a commitment to keep the Earth safe and livable for future generations…or let it continue to deteriorate. Businesses have more power to do either of these than any other institution in our society.
Is there really any choice to make?

To help you make the necessary changes, the EarthWorks Group will provide national referrals for "green" business consultants and environmental auditors.

For information, write to us at:

THE EARTHWORKS GROUP
1400 Shattuck Ave., #25
Berkeley, CA 94709

The Earthworks Group Recommends:

THE GREEN BUSINESS LETTER

If you like the information in this book but want to learn more, we recommend *The Green Business Letter*, a valuable monthly newsletter for companies that want to "go green."

Each issue of *The Green Business Letter* provides hands-on, how-to information that can help your company be both economical and ecological. For example, you'll learn about:
• Where to find low-cost recycled office products
• Ecological tax incentives for business
• Energy-saving upgrades for heating and air conditioning systems
• Industrial-strength green cleaners
• Environmental education programs for employees and executives
• CFC-free products
• How to conduct a green product audit
• Low-cost community environmental projects
• Products that can cut your lighting bill in half
• How to write and implement a company-wide environmental policy

Every issue features new products and services, meetings and conferences, book and article reviews ... and interviews with executives, managers, and employees who have helped their companies do their part for the planet.

Subscription price is $97 a year for 12 issues. For more information: *The Green Business Letter, 1526 Connecticut Ave. NW Washington, D.C. 20036 (202) 332-1700; (800) 955-GREEN.*

MORE BOOKS FROM EARTHWORKS PRESS

• *50 Simple Things You Can Do to Save the Earth*, by the EarthWorks Group. *Called "the environmental bible" by critics. A #1 best seller; more than 3 million copies sold.* $4.95.

• *The Recycler's Handbook*, by the EarthWorks Group. *Everything you need to know to make recycling a part of your life.* $4.95.

• *30 Simple Energy Things You Can Do to Save the Earth*, by the EarthWorks Group. *Practical tips for saving energy at home.* $3.95.

• *50 Simple Things Kids Can Do to Recycle*, by the EarthWorks Group. The sequel to the best selling *50 Simple Things Kids Can Do to Save the Earth. Kids wrote to us and asked for it; now here's the book that will teach them to recycle.* $5.95.

• *The Student Environmental Action Guide*, by the Student Environmental Action Coalition. The first environmental handbook written for college students, by college students. $4.95.

Available at bookstores, or from EarthWorks Press, 1400 Shattuck Ave. #25, Berkeley, CA 94709. (415) 841-5866. Add $1 per book, shipping and handling. Call for bulk rates.

INDEX